An Eclectic Life

An Eclectic Life

A memoir

By

Pat Holt

All rights reserved. No parts of this book may be used or reproduced in any manner whatsoever without written permission, except in the case of brief quotations embodied in critical articles or reviews.

Copyright © 2010 Pat Holt All rights reserved

Cover design © 2010 Karen Pummill-Neal All rights reserved

Burr Oak Publishing
www.burroakpublishing.com

Printed in the U.S.A.

ISBN 978-1451527674

Special thanks to the members of WOW for listening, my friends and relatives for reading and re-reading my stories and their encouragement.

Thanks also for the encouragement and help with editing of my friends.

I have changed the names of some of the people in the following pages to protect their privacy.

Others may have different versions of events, this book contains my memories the way I experienced them.

Little Patty in the field.

Table of Contents

The Early Days 1

Aunt Nettie 5

Uncle George 9

Seamstress 13

Turkey Farm Job 15

Marine Corps Time 17

Storm Window Factory 33

Working at Wassaic 35

Pat's IBM 39

Pat's Coffee Break 45

Merchandiser 53

My Summer Job 57

Cats In My Life 63

The Price of Ice Cream 69

My First House 71

Living In Archie 89

Political Me 103

Rebuilding Pearlington 107

My Tomatoes	119
The Dentist Visit	125
The Prize	131
My First Big Trip	139
Chicago Trip	145

Me at four years old.
The bosses big house in the background.

Me at one year old.

Road to barn and back fields.

Barn where we played

The big house where my father's boss lived.

Treavor Road

Green House

Second house we lived in at nursery.

Pine trees

First house we lived in at the nursery.

Sand pile

Crushed stone driveway

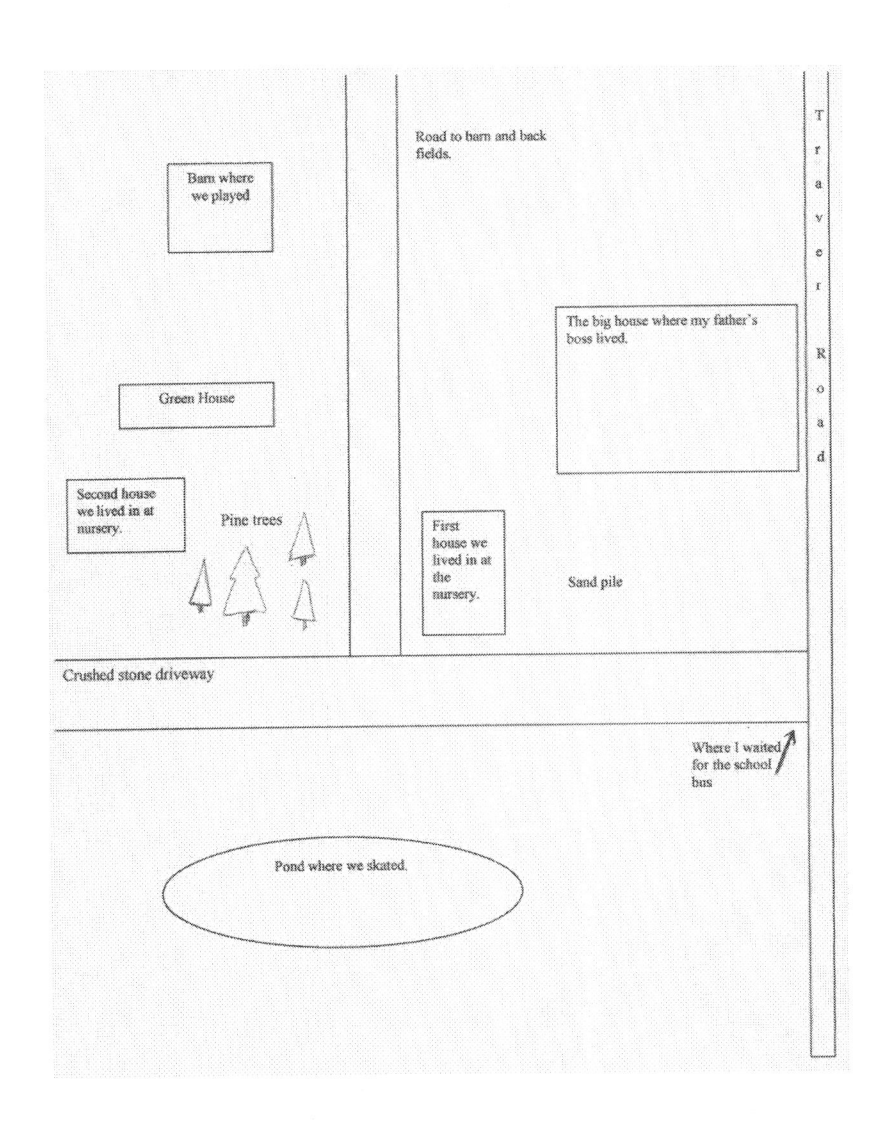

Where I waited for the school bus

Pond where we skated.

This is a map of where the early days took place.

The Early Days

When I was young, the little white house over the garage up the long crushed stone driveway where I lived with my family was the center of my world.

My sister was fifteen when I was born. During the early years of my life when she was in high school, she brought her friends home with her. They used to take me ice skating on the big pond across the driveway from our house. Ice skating was fun while I was skating, being pulled around the ice as a little girl by my sister and her friends, and being the center of attention. The things that I didn't like so much were that my ankles were weak, which meant that they bent over as I skated, so they hurt and I couldn't skate very well or fast. I fell down a lot. Maybe the worst thing in my memory about ice skating was when we went back into the house and my icy feet started to warm up. That's when the pain started. As I think about it now it is still vivid as it seemed that my toes hurt all the way up to my knees.

As I got a little older, I spent a lot of time alone playing in the sand pile that was near the front of my house. In the comics pages of the newspaper there were stories about imaginary little people called the "Teeny Weenie's." They were real to me as I made houses for them, and roads for them to drive on. I would landscape their houses with little stones and sticks, and have hours of fun with them.

Sometimes my Aunt Toddy would come to visit my mother and and bring my cousin Ronnie with her. We both liked to play in the sand pile. He seemed to me to have much better ideas for landscaping his houses and roads. Ronnie and I were almost the same age. I'm only about two months older than he is. As Ronnie and I got older we were allowed to play farther from the house, which is when we discovered the hay loft in the barn. We had lots of good times making forts with the bails of hay, and jumping into piles of it. One day while we were rearranging some hay bails, Ronnie swung the hay hook down onto a bail of hay at the same time I reached with my right hand. The curved hay hook dug into my right hand between my pinkie and ring finger! I'm sure I could see the bone for a while before the blood started. It was a very strange experience, since I don't remember it hurting at all. For a long time I used to look at that scar to be sure which was right and which was left. Now that seems pretty strange, I would think I should have known my left from my right by that age, somewhere around eleven I think.

Ronnie's and my next fun thing to do was to climb one of the pine trees near my house, and to go high enough that the tree would bend toward another tree. Then we would swing to the next tree, and have a great time swinging from pine tree to pine tree. It sure was fun, until we got home and got in trouble for all of the pine pitch that was on us and our clothes.

Sometime in my pre-teen years I tied a towel around my neck like a cape and jumped off that green house like Superman would. I didn't fly, just landed unhurt but embarrassed on the ground.

The place where I grew up was a wholesale tree nursery and my father was the foreman. I used to go with him to the green house sometimes and watch as he put little pieces of trees called "cuttings" into boxes of sand. First he would dip the cutting into water then into white powder that helped make the roots grow, and then he would stick them into the sand in straight rows. After these cuttings grew good root systems, they would be transplanted into bigger flats. Then they would be planted out in the fields when they got to be about a foot tall.

When these shrubs got big enough, they would be sold to retail stores or smaller wholesale nurseries.

The man who owned the nursery was a New York City doctor so he spent most weekdays away from Pleasant Valley. His wife had red hair, held herself stiffly, and most of the time, it seems to me, she carried around a mixed drink. I remember my mother calling it a Tom Collins. Dr. and Mrs. Rawls had two children: a boy named Bryant who was near my age, and a girl named Janet who was a couple of years older. Their house was the largest house I had ever seen. To add to the size of the house there was an addition of the end they called the "West Wing," which was made up of six or eight bedrooms with a hallway down the middle. They had a black butler/cook named William to help take care of the house and prepare food for the large parties they occasionally had. Sometimes Bryant and Janet would let me play with them, but mostly I was ignored by them.

The driveway in front of our house seemed very long when I was young. I used to have to walk down it all alone to get the school bus, but after I was grown and went back to see it again it wasn't very long at all. The driveway was covered with crushed stones that were about 1 inch around and had very rough, pointy edges. It seemed to be very important to me that I could run down the driveway bare foot. I always wanted to be like a superhero and since flying off the greenhouse didn't work, running on crushed stone was the closest I could come to a super power.

Pat Holt

Aunt Nettie

My mother's oldest sister was named Henrietta, but everyone always called her Nettie. My aunt Nettie was really nice, and was involved in lots of groups. She was a member of the Women of the Moose, which is a community service organization, the American Legion Auxiliary and the Eastern Star, which is a part of the Masons. She was the pianist for the Women of the Moose and the Order of the Eastern Star. She used to make corn pancakes, for me, using real corn that she would cut off the cob she also used to can bread and butter pickles.

Her first husband was my uncle Herb. They were married and divorced before I was born. They had one daughter, my cousin Maude. Maude was about 20 years older than me, so it was always hard to think of her as a cousin, and not an aunt. Uncle Herb's last name was Wilbur, his family owned a lot of land in Pleasant Valley and had a road named after them. When I was growing up Uncle Herb and Maude lived in his family home on Wilbur Road, it was very large and full of antique furniture.

As you entered the house there was a small entryway, it was a place where you could leave your boots or coat so you wouldn't have to bring them into the house. To the right as you entered there was a kitchen, in the kitchen Maude had a refrigerator that she was buying on an installment plan, she had to put quarters into a device attached to it, to keep it running. I don't remember how many or how often. I always remember the whole house as being very crowded with furniture. Whenever anyone in the family died it seemed that Maude got their furniture. On the first floor there was also a dining room, a parlor, a sunroom, and a living room, upstairs there were bedrooms and a bathroom. There was a piano in the living room which Maude would sometimes play and sing along as she played. She was a gifted singer, and family lore is that she could have been a famous opera singer if she had tried, but she decided to stay in Pleasant Valley and live in the family home.

She fell in love with a married man and devoted her life to him. They had regular dates on Thursday evenings, and maybe other times when he could get away. For years this affair went on, and she always thought that someday he would leave his wife to marry her. I know that because she told me the day he died when I stopped to see her. She couldn't even go to his funeral, this man whom she loved for so many years without being able to marry.

As far as I remember she never had a job until after his death and after her father re-married. Actually her father's marriage is a story on its own. My mother's youngest brother died in 1959, and his widow became friendlier with Uncle Herb, over time they started seeing each other romantically, they decided to get married, to each other. It was a rather awkward relationship when it had to be explained. She had six kids by her first husband and some of her kids called him "Uncle-Daddy", since he had always been their uncle and now he was their step-father. After this Maude had to get a job, she worked at the local grade school in the office as far as I know until she retired. Maude never married and was a little eccentric, she raised chickens and sometimes in the winter when it was very cold she would bring the chickens into the house to keep them warm and safe. After retirement, since she didn't have enough money to afford her family home she sold it, but had an arrangement where she could remain living in a specially built section of it

As I grew up and married and moved around I lost touch with her until a point after she had to move out of her home due to problems with the people she sold it to, she was living in the home of a lady who was renting out rooms to senior citizens. When I visited she seemed to be very happy there since she could have her cat with her and everyone there seemed to be very friendly. About a year before her death in 1999 when she was in a nursing home my son and I went to visit her again and even though she was living in one room she had made friends and the residents and staff both enjoyed her beautiful voice. I'm really glad that we took the time to make those visits so that we could get re-acquainted before her death.

  Aunt Nettie's second husband was my uncle Nat. They lived in Poughkeepsie at 13 Eighmie Terrace until about 1960 when a major highway construction project was undertaken by the city, at that time they moved to Hyde Park. It was from her that I learned that the roads in the city were referred to as streets, not roads like in the country, it was very important to her so she corrected me whenever I got it wrong. Sometimes I would go to spend the night at her house. Their house in Poughkeepsie was different in many ways from the houses of anyone else I knew, starting with the street which was made of cement and the sidewalk right in front, there wasn't any lawn, there were stairs up to the porch which had a stuffed couch, called a glider, because it glided back and forth. We didn't have anything like this back in Pleasant Valley. Our roads were either dirt or "black top" which I think was macadam, the only place I knew of sidewalks was in the center of town along Main Street, and a short way along North Avenue. All of the houses along these streets in Pleasant Valley had at least a small lawn and sometimes some flowers. They also had a different heating system, there was a large metal grate in the living room floor with a furnace under and that is where the heat came up that heated the whole house. In the winter it got very hot and would burn the bottom of your feet if you stepped on it, it was pretty uncomfortable to step on even in the summer with bare feet. The bathroom was upstairs and the toilet was another thing what was really different from what I was used to. Instead of a normal tank to hold water right behind the toilet, the tank was up closer to the ceiling, and there was a chain attached that was pulled to flush the toilet. Sometimes when I would come to visit we would go to the movies at a theater called the Astor Theater, it was only about 2 or 3 blocks away so we would walk. That theater later was closed and re-opened as a restaurant called The Chance that had live music, as an adult I saw Dr. Hook, Chris Kristofferson, and many other famous artists there. It was always fun to go and reminisce about my days as a youngster watching movies when it was a movie theater.

  Aunt Nettie died in 1962 at the age of 69, Uncle Nat died April 22, 1960 on their 21st wedding anniversary, and he was only 66 years old.

Uncle George

Fire Island is located along the southern edge of Long Island, New York. It is about 31 miles long and very narrow, and varies from 0.1 miles to 0.25 miles wide[1]. The only way onto the island is by the five mile ride on the ferry from Sayville, New York. The part of the island where I had been staying does not allow cars, because there aren't any roads. The walkways are board walks built up over the sandy land. The fire department uses a golf cart sized fire truck and the garbage is collected from each house along the boardwalk with the golf cart garbage truck. My friend's home is on the beach side of the island and her front yard boarders the clothing optional beach.

I stood near the dock on the hot summer day as I was leaving from a relaxing weekend with my friends, my thoughts suddenly turned to my Uncle George. I could picture him boarding the train from New York City and getting the ferry at Sayville to come over to Fire Island to spend time with his friends at the beach, sitting in the sun that he loved so much, I am sure that he kept his clothes on. Probably he wore his suit pants, and his white ribbed undershirt similar to what he wore when he sat in the sun at our house.

He was my my mother's oldest brother and had lived in New York City all of his adult life. He was born April 12, 1896 over his father's store in Pleasant Valley, New York and grew up in Pleasant Valley. He moved to New York City after he served in the Navy during World War I. Uncle George loved sitting outside in the sun, and when he came to Pleasant Valley to visit my parents he always sat outside in the lawn chair to sun himself. He had shiny silver hair which was thin, and he always

---

[1] Information on size of Fire Island taken from Wikipedia, the free encyclopedia http://en.wikipedia.org/wiki/Fire_island,_New_York

wore it combed straight back and held in place with some hair product of the day. I don't know what he used but I do know that he smelled good; I think it was Old Spice because I remember seeing those bottles with his luggage when he came to visit. He was a little taller than my mother but much thinner. He always dressed very nicely with suit pants, nice shirts and jackets. His hands were soft more like my mothers than rough like my fathers, and he buffed his nicely manicured nails. He worked in an office in New York City at the Addressograph Company, where he made metal plates for imprinting names and addresses on mass mailings.

It was always a big happy event when Uncle George was coming to visit. My mother, father and I would pile into our car, and daddy would drive us to the train station in Poughkeepsie, New York to pick him up. Uncle George would get off the train carrying his brown leather suitcase. I would always ask him how long he was going to stay, not because I wanted him to leave, but because I wanted him to stay a long time. He was so kind and gentle, and I loved him the best of all my uncles. When we got back home he would open his suitcase and he would always have a new dollar for me, and some chocolate candy from the Schafts candy store in New York City. We would stop on the way home from the train station to get some coffee cake for us all to share. He really liked sweets so we had plenty when he visited. Most of the times that he visited we would go out to dinner at the Smith Brothers restaurant in Poughkeepsie, and I would have the "Mary's Little Lamb Chop." Now as I think about that name I wouldn't want to eat it. Sometimes we would go to a Chinese restaurant that had little cups with out handles for the tea. I can remember turning the cup around and around looking for the handle.

I didn't realize it when I was very young, but Uncle George had a wonderful dry sense of humor. Even though

Uncle George loved to eat and ate very well he could only eat small amounts at a time and he was very thin. He said when it was windy in New York City he used to have to hang onto the light polls.

My mother with Uncle George in 1956 on one of his trips to Pleasant Valley to visit.

Uncle George in his New York City apartment after he got his new teeth.

This picture is a Polaroid and on the back he wrote "Ultra Brite" Ad; showing off my new teeth! Also noted on the back of the picture is that he weighted 65 pounds. Ultra Brite is a tooth paste marketed by Colgate-Palmolive. Uncle George died at St. Claire's Hospital in New York City, he had gotten knocked down and broke his hip while shopping and never recovered.

I still miss his dry wit and his positive attitude.

Pat Holt

Seamstress

While I was married I did a lot of sewing; I made most of my daughter Karen's clothes, some for my son Tony, and a lot of my own and I even made boxers for my husband, Frank. Little girls are easy to sew for, and boxers are pretty easy to make. I would make dresses for Karen, and matching clothes for myself. When Tony was small I made him some pants with elastic waste bands, but once he needed zippers I stopped. I wasn't very good at putting zippers into men's pants so I didn't make any pants for Frank or Tony.

When our neighbor Linda was planning her wedding and didn't have much money she asked me to make her wedding dress and bridesmaids' dresses, so I did. It wasn't really very hard. I just went with her to the store and bought the Butterick pattern that she chose. She was the same size as the pattern and the material she chose was easy to work with. The bridesmaids' also fit their dresses without problems.

Since I was doing so well at all of the projects I attempted, I thought it naturally followed that I could do some sewing for people around town and make some extra money for our family. It seemed like a simple plan to me, I just needed to find customers. I knew a local woman in Pleasant Valley who did sewing for money. I asked her if she had any extra customers that needed sewing or alterations would she refer them to me she agreed and I was ready to get started.

The first customer she referred to me was a very nice lady, but her proportions were rather unconventional. Her bust was rather large, so she needed a large size for the front of her dress. Her back was very narrow in contrast to her front. The first obstacle to be overcome would be to alter the pattern to fit. Her hips were even larger than her bust so the dress had to be enlarged for that area, too.

To compound the problem the material that she chose was very expensive and slippery. It was some kind of silk or rayon blend; I don't remember which. Since I had taken on the task, I felt that I must finish it, and I did. The amount of time it took was way more than I had expected when I quoted her the price, or when I agreed to do the job. If you calculate the amount of time I spent and the amount of money I earned, it was probably about 5 cents per hour or maybe less. I didn't even allow for the stress connected with the project.

It certainly was a learning experience in many ways. I learned I wasn't cut out to be a seamstress for hire. I learned that when you ask someone for recommendations, the people they suggest might be the customers that they don't want to do work with because the project might not be profitable.

Although Jane liked her dress very much my career as a seamstress for hire came to an end. After that short attempt at being a seamstress for money I gave up the idea and went back to making boxers for my husband and clothes for my daughter.

Turkey Farm Job

About 5 years after my sister's death in 1947, my brother-in-law married a lady named Mickey, who I have always referred to as my sister-in-law. They lived near us in Pleasant Valley. I visited them a lot. When I was 16 and Mickey, who was an office manager for a local turkey farm needed office help for the Thanksgiving and Christmas holidays she would hire me.

The main business of the turkey farm where she worked was to ship frozen or fresh turkeys as gifts to employees of various companies. Some companies were very big, like P. Lorillard, the parent company of Kent cigarettes, and Lipton or the smaller companies or individuals.

In the beginning the turkeys were raised on the farm in Washington Hollow, New York, about 5 miles east of Pleasant Valley. Local people were hired to kill, clean and pluck the turkeys. My mother and aunt were among the workers. This was my mother's first and only job outside the home. Their job was finished when all the plucking was done.

We started by typing labels as soon as orders started to appear prior to Thanksgiving. As it got closer to Thanksgiving and the shipping room was set up, each turkey had to be put into a cardboard box and packed with shredded paper. All employees worked packing turkeys. It was cold in the shipping room and we got plenty of paper cuts since it was hard to pack the paper around the turkey with gloves on, because they would get stuck in the packing. The box was then topped off with shredded red or green cellophane, a gift card was placed into the box and a shipping label attached. Then the box would continue rolling down the assembly line to the sorting area where it would be assigned a shipping area according to the UPS or Post Office map. The first year most of the boxes went to New York City, and other places within about a one hundred mile range . As soon as Thanksgiving was over we got started on Christmas.

The hours were very long. Mickey was dedicated to her job, and we would work from very early in the morning until late at night. On weekends and during school vacations I would spend the night at her house and we would fall asleep to Johnny Mathis singing Christmas songs. I continued this job every holiday season for three years.

During the shipping times when we finished, the owners of the Turkey Farm would take us to a nice local restaurant for dinner to celebrate, but no one ordered turkey!

Marine Corps Time

After graduating from Arlington High School in Poughkeepsie, New York in June, 1958, I didn't find any employment I wanted around home. I couldn't afford college, and I didn't want to get married right away. It seemed logical to me that I should join the service.

I started out with the idea of joining the Navy because they offered the most opportunity for different fields of training, and also my father had been in the Navy during World War I. I went to the Navy recruitment office, at the Post Office building in Poughkeepsie. Everything was going fine until I tried to read the eye chart and failed. My eyesight was not correctable to 20/20, so I failed the physical. The Marine Corps recruiter had been eavesdropping; he saw my sadness at being rejected. He quietly called me aside and told me if I would sign up for the Marine Corps, he would help me with the eye chart. He did that by standing behind me and whispering the letters to me. I passed, and I was recruited into the United States Marine Corps. I was scheduled to leave from the train station in Poughkeepsie, March 5, 1959, change trains at Penn Station in New York City and have a sleeping compartment, all expenses paid to Florence, South Carolina.

I don't know if I was more excited or nervous. I had never been away from home for any length of time. I don't remember much of the trip south; it is all kind of a blur. A Marine Corps bus took us from the train station in Florence to the Marine Corps training center at Parris Island, South Carolina.

I arrived at the barracks surprised and happy to see that the other women were as young and as scared as I was. I guess I thought they would be much older.

The barracks was a one-story brick building. As you entered the center of the building, to the left the sergeants and other non-commissioned officers had their sleeping quarters, to the right, was our quarters.

As you walked down the cement-floored hallway, the door on the right was to the laundry room, with washers, ironing boards, and sinks for hand washings. The dryers weren't the same as modern dryers where hot air comes in and the clothes are twirled around. They had tall drawers with metal rods where clothes would be hung, and then the drawer would be slid back into the heated chamber. As you can imagine our clothes did not come out of there wrinkle free and soft, so everything had to be ironed. As we ironed each item, we had spray starch and bottles of water to spray on them to help get the wrinkles out. Our uniforms had to be wrinkle free at inspection time. This was extremely important since we had to have daily inspections, and if one person failed we would all lose privileges.

A little farther down the hallway on the left was the bathroom and shower area. The toilets were in stalls with doors similar to the ones in the public ladies rooms of today. I'm not sure how many there were, maybe ten, five in each direction as you entered the room. The wall straight ahead as you walked into the room was lined with sinks, which were where we brushed our teeth and where the black girls would heat their curling irons. I remember the smell of burning hair seemed to overpower everything else.

Farther into the room and to the right there was the shower room area. The floor there was also cement. There were dividers for privacy while showering, but there was also an open area for dressing. This open area doubled as our smoking area.

Continuing down the hall past the laundry room and the bathroom was an area called the "squad bay." This was where we lived. At the entrance there was a common area with couches, chairs and coffee tables. This was our living room, or family room. Through this area to the left and right were our cubicles. We slept on bunk beds, two of us to each cubicle, and each cubical was separated by tall green lockers and dressers that held our uniforms. Foot lockers for our folded uniforms were under our bunks.

As we began our boot camp experience some of us needed hair cuts to comply with the rule in force at that time. The rule was that your hair could touch but not cover your collar. There were beauticians for the white girls, but since we were in South Carolina and it was 1959 the white beauticians would not work on the black girls. Much to my shock and dismay the black girls were given a pair of very large scissors and told to cut each others' hair! They obeyed without question; actually they didn't seem as offended as I did. I can still remember my shock at the big unwieldy scissors that they were given.

Each day during boot camp we would have to get up very early, and be ready for inspection of ourselves and our clothes by 6 a.m., and then we would march to the mess hall for breakfast. After breakfast we would march back to our barracks for inspection, we all had to have clean pressed clothes, and the proper red lipstick, which had to be the same color red as the piping on our dress uniforms. There couldn't be any dust or dirt anywhere, even up under the beds or the spaces up under the dressers behind the legs. The cement floors were mopped and buffed with an electric buffer. Our beds had to be made in the standard military way with extra tight sheets and blankets, and specially folded corners. I never remember anyone bouncing a quarter on the beds like in the movies, but they were expected to be stretched tight enough that a quarter could be bounced.

If all of these conditions were met to our sergeant's satisfaction, the smokers would be allowed a ten minute smoke break. Our smoking area was in the open area at the front of the shower room. We were allowed to smoke cigarettes up to four times a day, usually ten minutes at a time. We would have a chance to smoke after meals and once in the evening if we were really lucky. Someone would get a dustpan, and we would go to the shower room with it, and all huddle around and inhale as much smoke as we could in as short a time. Cigarettes get very hot when you are taking such quick, long drags, so I used to light two cigarettes at the same time and smoke first one then the other. The dustpan would have to be emptied and put away by the end of the ten minutes. The area would then be checked to make sure there were no ashes or butts around or we would lose our smoking privilege for next time.

Smoke time was a privilege, or not smoking was a punishment, however you want to think about it since everyone had to pass inspection of our clothes and our bunk area in order for us to be able to have smoking time. At the time, I smoked, so I had to suffer when others didn't do their jobs. This type of punishment was supposed to instill teamwork, but I saw it as creating animosity toward those who didn't do their jobs.

Most of our meals were like that, march to the mess hall, march back, and hope we could get to smoke.

It wasn't until the early 1960's that women were equal to men and were allowed to do more jobs. Although we didn't learn to handle rifles or have hand-to-hand combat training, for some reason that I'm not sure of, we did get to experience chlorine and tear gas in the gas chamber and learn how to put on a gas mask. After instructions we were taken to a long building. First we walked through the gas-filled building with our gas masks on. After that experience we entered again without masks and put on our masks after the gas was dispersed, and continued through the building and out the other end. We saw a movie and were told about nerve gas, and the syringes that male Marines carry to counteract it, but we didn't have to go as far as experiencing that.

There was a story that I believe to be true of a platoon sergeant who had taken his platoon through the swamps and several didn't obey his commands. They were lost in the quick sand, so it was drummed into us that we must obey commands and that as Marines we were the best at everything.

There was also the story of the soldier who slapped a sand flea that was biting him while he was on a Pacific Island during World War II, and the noise of that slap gave away his position to the enemy, causing him and his whole platoon to be killed. Therefore, we were never allowed to slap sand fleas. One time we were encouraged to wear makeup for a drill. We soon realized that was to draw the sand fleas to us so we could practice letting them swarm around and bite us without hitting them.

To condition us to obey commands, we were made to march. Even though we were not trained for any combat skills we were still conditioned to obey without thinking. When we weren't marching or doing calisthenics, we were in classes on Marine Corps history. We learned that since the Marine Corps was created on November 10, 1775, at Tun Tavern in Philadelphia, they always fought with valor and determination. They were tougher than any other fighters. Between the World Wars, the Marine Corps was headed by Commandant John A. Lejeune, and under his leadership, the Corps studied and developed amphibious techniques that were of great use fighting and capturing the Japanese on many small islands during World War II. I have forgotten most of the details of the history, but I do remember the pride that was instilled in all of us.

Our mission was to replace the men in offices when they were needed in combat. We marched three to four hours each day. While marching it is important to strike the ground with your heel for the sound and so that you look sharp. That is why there were a lot of foot problems, from pounding our heels on black top as we marched. When we were marching on the drill fields, I remember seeing the male Marines. They had it harder than we did. No one ever hit any of us, but there were always some of them with bandages on their heads.

One of the things that we were told was that the women in the Marine Corps were called Women Marines to not take the name Marine away from us. Unlike the women in the Navy, who are called WAVES (Women Accepted for Volunteer Emergency Service)[2], or the women in the Army who are called WACs (Women's Army Corps).

In the beginning of boot camp there were about fifty of us. Over the period of training about half were discharged due to physical problems, which were mostly foot related or mental problems, which was from the stress. The ability to complete the training when so many couldn't added to our pride at completing boot camp and graduating.

Everyone who completed basic training went on to General Office Procedure School, which lasted four more weeks and was still at Parris Island. This school consisted of classroom training, marching, and more Marine Corps history, in case we didn't have enough pride.

During that time we had more freedom, including freedom to spend time out of our barracks and around the base every other night for a couple of hours. We still had to march to

---

[2] a World War II era division of the U.S. Navy that consisted entirely of women

and from meals together, and had daily inspections. We didn't have cars so we couldn't go far, but I got to go on liberty off the base two times. The first weekend I went to Beaufort, South Carolina, the town closest to the base with members of my platoon. The other weekend I went with a group of friends to Savannah, Georgia, about 50 miles away. We drank quite a bit while we were there. The only places we visited were bars. Before I left Parris Island, I returned to Savannah with my platoon to march in a Memorial Day Parade.

During the time we were together, we became a very united group of women, and also very sure that being a Woman Marine meant that we were the best of the best, and we were very proud of that. "The Few. The Proud. The Marines. Semper Fi; Always Faithful"

When it was time to graduate and go home I was in the group that was to go by bus. We were taken to the bus station in Beaufort, South Carolina. As we entered the bus station on that hot late-spring day, the black girls among us were told that they could not wait for the bus inside the bus station. It didn't matter that we were United States Marines. When our friends weren't allowed in the bus station, we went outside and waited with them.

It was another of the many instances of segregation and bigotry I encountered in the south. Back home in Pleasant Valley there weren't many black people that I knew of, and the ones that I did know were just like me, and were treated that way. My mother and father, were very good friends with a black lady named Georgie; she was a wonderful lady and the first black person I knew. Actually she was the only one I did know until I went to school. When we went to the neighboring city and saw black people I thought they must be her relatives. Therefore the idea of segregation was strange to me

The bus ride home was uneventful. While I was home my boyfriend asked me to marry him. I told him no, that I couldn't marry anyone but a Marine. I believed that only someone who had survived Marine Corps boot camp was good enough for me.

After a two-week leave, I was to be stationed at Camp Lejeune, North Carolina. While I was away in Boot Camp my Uncle Fred had died, and left his wife, my aunt Toddy some money. She needed a car so she bought a canary yellow Ford Fairlane convertible with a black top, a very snazzy car. She had a new car, and I needed a ride to North Carolina. My parents decided that we would all make the trip together. My mother, father, aunt Toddy, nephew Gary and cousin Brent, and I, drove the 663 miles from Pleasant Valley, New York to Camp Lejeune, North Carolina. Gary and Brent were 12 years old at the time. We drove down through New Jersey and took the Delaware Bay Ferry, which was quite an experience. I once again saw discrimination, this time in the form of "colored" drinking fountains. I still didn't understand it, and was appalled by it. The trip on the ferry was long, and rough. It seemed like it was at least an hour. I know there were times when we were in the middle and couldn't see land in any direction. The bridge-tunnel system that has replaced it is 19 miles long, so I guess that is how far our ride was.

On the way we stopped at some cabins to spend the night, and we stopped to eat at picnic areas along the highway. There were just places to pull off with picnic tables and garbage cans, unlike the rest areas of today. They were also not as crowded, nor did they have public rest rooms.

The barracks at Camp Lejeune were very similar to the ones at Parris Island, with one exception. At the front end of our squad bay near a door there was an area set aside for four Corps WAVES. Those were the nurses' aids that were in the Navy.

An Eclectic Life

The Marine Corps did not have medical personnel; we were supported by Navy doctors and nurses.

I was stationed at Camp Lejeune for the remainder of my three year enlistment. Mostly I worked in a men's company office except the times when I had to have "mess duty."

In the office job I was the pay and discharge clerk. I gathered information and filled in the discharge papers and got information prepared for when they were discharged from the Marine Corps. One set of forms that had to be filled in was the DD-214, there were three copies needed. This was before the day of computers, so carbon paper was used between the pages, and there couldn't be any mistakes in the typing.

Mess duty was something that we did at least once a year or sometimes as a punishment for minor infractions of rules. It consisted of getting up very early and going to the mess hall to help prepare meals and cleaning up after. After each meal we had to move all of the tables and benches out of the mess hall and pour buckets of soapy water onto the cement floor, then scrub with brushes, rinse and use squeegees to push the water into the drain hole, and replace the tables and benches for the next meal.

There were many similar brick barracks throughout the base, and each contained a company of men, and they were grouped in battalions. There were bars called "Slop Shoots" through out the camp, but the only one that allowed enlisted women who were not officers or non-commissioned officers was the one next to our barracks. There was always a line of men on the sidewalk outside the door waiting to be escorted in, since they could only enter when escorted by one of us. In these "Slop Shoots" hard liquor wasn't served, only beer and soda, but lots of it. There was also a juke box with all the popular music of the time, a bar, a few tables and chairs, and a large dance floor. During most of my first year I don't think I ever got past my local "Slop Shoot," and I don't think I ever bought a drink for myself.

After a while it became the place to go during the week. But on weekends when we had more time we would go into Jacksonville, North Carolina. My challenge to myself was to drink in every bar in Jacksonville on one night. My problem was that I kept forgetting what happened when I drank, so I don't know if I ever met my challenge.

I had another problem with alcohol, and now I think of it as an allergy. As I drank, I would get hives. They would start out as red blotches on my hands, neck, and face, then blend together to cause me to look pretty strange for a while, then the redness would fade away along with my memory. It never occurred to me not to drink because of this problem, but I wasn't ever shy about talking about it.

Sometimes when we went to J-Ville, which is what we called Jacksonville, we would get a hotel room, and then go to an ABC store, which is where you could buy liquor. We'd buy some vodka and get some orange juice from the grocery store. We would put them in our hotel room. We would then head out into J-Ville and hit the bars. One of our favorite night spots was "The Band Box." They had a band, and we would all get drunk and request the band to play our favorite song, "Boney Maroney" over and over. We especially liked that song because the name of our commanding officer was Captain Maroney. After the bar closed, we would go to our hotel room and continue drinking.

One of the other fun things I remember doing was going to the beach. We used to go to Onslow Beach, North Carolina, because it was only about 14 miles away. I would join some friends who had a car, since I didn't have a driver's license, and we would stop at an ABC store to get some cases of Carlings Black Label beer. The reason I remember the brand of beer is that I have a picture of myself with a couple of friends on the beach with a pile of Carlings Black Label beer cans. I didn't do much swimming except one time I remember walking out into the ocean and then the next thing I remember is sitting by the fire drying out. Mostly we would just build a fire and sit around it and drink.

In the spring of 1961 I made what was considered an outstanding comment in the "If You Ask Me" column of the Camp Lejeune Globe, the base newspaper. Whatever it was it impressed the commanding officer of Company "L" Tigers, 3rd Battalion, 2nd Marines so much that I was invited to receive an award of being named the "Tigress of the month" and I was given a certificate, and review of their formal guard mount. What this meant was that I went to their company area and watched as they marched past. When they stopped I could walk between the rows and inspect as they saluted with their rifles. It was a really great honor. I also had these pictures taken:

There were some things I didn't like about the Marine Corps, like every month even after boot camp we had to have inspections where everything was checked for cleanliness, and all of our gear was checked. We needed to maintain at least two complete sets of uniforms in perfect condition. To prove that we maintained them properly, we had an inspection referred to as "junk-on-the-bunk." For this inspection all required items of clothing had to be folded and displayed on our bunks in the prescribed manner. That was one of my least favorite things that I had to do; it seemed like such a waste of time.

Other unpleasant memories were the times when there was a purge of lesbians. Every once in a while since homosexuals were not allowed to serve in the Marine Corps, there would be list of women who the officers in charge determined were lesbians. This list was provided to the Commanding Officer by informers within our company. We would be called into formation and the lesbians would be called out and given an "Other Than Honorable Discharge." That is a category between a General Discharge which you get if you separate under honorable conditions, without a sufficiently meritorious military record to deserve an Honorable Discharge and a Bad Conduct Discharge which you only get after a court-martial. There was never any other proof needed or trial, just the word of these informers, and action was taken.

I used to go home on weekends sometimes, mostly long weekends, but sometimes regular ones. I would get a ride up to New York City and get the train from Grand Central Station to Poughkeepsie, and take a taxi to my home in Pleasant Valley or sometimes my father would pick me up at the train station. Most of the time I knew the guys that I got rides with but not always. The Base rule was that you could go anywhere on weekend liberty within 600 miles of the base. Most of us didn't follow that rule.

On one nice spring weekend, when my Aunt Donna was getting married, and I wanted to go, I talked my friends Sam and Sonja into driving the 663 miles up to Pleasant Valley, New York to the wedding. We brought our dress blue uniforms because we were very proud of who we were, and wanted my friends and family to see. Sam drove his Pontiac Catalina straight through. I think he did take a little nap after we arrived, but it couldn't have been very long. We got dressed in our uniforms and looked really sharp for the wedding. After the wedding, we had a few beers and a few more drinks of whatever was offered. It was mid-afternoon and we decided that we should go back to my house, which was only about 3 or 4 miles from the wedding and rest so we could go out partying some more in the evening. Sam was speeding down the road as "Blue Moon" was blasted on the radio. As we hit a bump in the road, the car couldn't make the turn and I heard the weeds and dirt hit the car as we left the road. The next I knew we were upside down with the windshield broken. As I crawled out through the windshield I was telling Sam to get out. Sonja had been thrown out of the car. We had all been sitting in the front seat and had not been wearing seatbelts. I don't even think cars had seat belts back then. There was a house across the street, so I went over to ask them to call an ambulance for my friends. I thought I was very calm until I started to knock on the door, and my hand became like it belonged to someone else and banged uncontrollably on the front door. When the lady came to the door, she said her husband was calling the ambulance. It came soon after. We were taken to the local hospital. I had cuts on both my knees. Sam and Sonja both had some head injuries, and other bumps and bruises. We were supposed to stay overnight in the hospital but decided that we had to get back to the Base on time so we wouldn't get into trouble. My cousin Babs and her husband Nick drove us back to Camp Lejeune. We arrived on time, but we did get caught for being outside the 600 mile limit on weekend liberty because of our stay in the hospital. We were given disciplinary actions called "Article 15" that consisted of going in front of the Battalion Commander and getting some kind of sentence. We all got some restriction to base and a suspended sentence of reduction in rank. The "everyone does it" defense didn't work. From that I learned a rule is a rule, and if you get caught it doesn't matter if everybody else does it.

As I settled into a routine of the "Slop Shoot" during the week, and J-Ville or Pleasant Valley on the weekend time went by. One night in the line for the "Slop Shoot" there was a very handsome man with dark brown eyes, and black hair. His name was Frank, and I let him escort me inside. I think it was love at first sight. We started going steady right away, and soon after he asked me to marry him. Of course I said yes. He was a Marine, had been in the Marine Corps for almost 9 years, and was as gung-ho as I was. I brought him home to meet my family and they hit it off right away. He was certainly a charmer and had quite a gift of gab. Finding out that he was about to be court-martialed for being a bigamist didn't stop me. I believed his story that he thought he was divorced from Olivia when he married Barbara, and that he truly loved me. His first wife, Olivia was in Arizona, which is where he had lived when he enlisted, and I'm not sure where Barbara was from or whatever happened to her. He did end up getting a court-martial and spending time in the brig. Because of the intervention of Barry Goldwater, the senator from Arizona, he was released from the brig and discharged from the Marine Corps with a General Discharge.

I left the Marine Corps in March 1962, and went back to Pleasant Valley. When Frank was discharged, he also came to Pleasant Valley and stayed with my cousin Babs and her husband Nick until July 1963, when we got married. We moved into a nice little cottage and expected to live happily ever after.

    I had found my Marine.

Storm Window Factory

Sometime during 1974 I worked in the window section of a factory in Butler, Missouri where aluminum storm windows and doors were made.

The aluminum sections came in long lengths, so we used large very loud saws to cut them to fit desired size windows. My job was called a "Peener." There was an assembly line, with cut sides on a conveyer belt. It wasn't the kind that moves automatically like in the famous Lucy and Ethel candy factory, just rollers to make the pieces move easier. My job was to choose two pieces, hold them firmly together at the angled end, and push the foot peddle which would bring the automatic ball peen hammer down to permanently join the two pieces, turn and attach the others, until a square or rectangle frame was made. There was a guide on the machine so that the corners were held square, and the hammer struck the aluminum piece in the proper place. Square window forms were easy, but for rectangles the order of the pieces was very important and must be chosen carefully or the window parts wouldn't fit together. The pieces had to be fitted long, short, long, short to make a perfect rectangle.

We all belonged to a union, and as I remember it was a chapter of the UAW (United Auto Workers). Because of our union membership there were strict rules, and bells to tell us when to start work for the day, bells when it was time for starting and stopping our breaks, our lunch, and at quitting time. We were very well organized in that respect. We had dues automatically removed from our checks each week along with a one dollar donation any time someone died. We all thought it must be for anyone in the entire union who died, since there were many weeks when one dollar was removed and we didn't know of anyone dying. I am not sure of any benefit we got from the union, except the bells.

When it was time to renew our contract and we wanted a raise, the union representatives met with management and we did not get a raise. The union seemed to always side with the management. At the time we were getting paid a little over minimum wage, which at the time was $2.00 an hour. It was probably due to the union that we got anything over the minimum wage, but at the time we didn't think they did anything for us except take dues and and extra one dollar almost every week.

The job was pretty boring as you might expect. Sometimes as a change of pace from "peening," I worked as a spliner, that job entailed forcing a rubber spline[3] into the grove in the window frame to keep the screen in place.

No matter what the job inside that factory, there was always the shrill whine of the saws cutting the aluminum pieces. It never occurred to me that I should wear ear protection, and I'm sure that is the cause for some of my hearing loss. That job was my only experience with a union so it also caused me to be skeptical of Unions.

---

[3] **Spline** (from Bob Vila glossary) (1) A flat key or strip that fits into a groove or slot between two parts. Alternately, the groove or slot into which it fits.

Working at Wassaic

I graduated from LPN school in Nevada, Missouri, in 1976. Shortly after, with the help of my ex-husband I loaded up my Country Squire station wagon and a U-Haul with all of our belongings, and brought my two kids, Karen and Tony back to my home town of Pleasant Valley, New York. I took the exam in New York and got my LPN license. At the time there were more LPN's than there were jobs for them. I applied at a local hospital where I would have taken a job in the housekeeping department, but I was turned down because I was over qualified! I was able to get a job in a kitchen working and cleaning at an adult care facility, which for some reason I wasn't over qualified for. While I worked there, I looked for something else, where I could make more money.

I got a job at the Harlem Valley Psychiatric Center in Dover, New York. In 1975 the *Willowbrook Consent Decree* was signed. [4] Because of this, conditions had to be improved at

---

[4] (From Wikipedia) In early 1972, Geraldo Rivera, then an investigative reporter for television station WABC-TV in New York City, conducted a series of investigations at Willowbrook (on the heels of a previous series of articles in the *Staten Island Advance* and *Staten Island Register* newspapers), uncovering a host of deplorable conditions, including overcrowding, inadequate sanitary facilities, and physical and sexual abuse of residents by members of the school's staff. Rivera later appeared on the nationally televised Dick Cavett Show with film of patients at the school. In 1975, a *Willowbrook Consent Decree* was signed. This committed New York State to

all Psychiatric Centers in New York State, as part of that several buildings had to be rebuilt. While that took place the residents were housed at Wassaic Psychiatric Center a few miles away. More workers were needed to care for the residents. Because I was an LPN, I was hired for the third shift, 11 PM to 7 AM, as a therapy aid during the week and I replaced the RN on weekends. I could have had a job in the infirmary as an LPN, but there didn't seem to be any future there, so I chose the Therapy Aide/RN position. It was my first experience working as a nurse, and my first experience working with that population. During my training I had worked in a nursing home. While I held that job there weren't any medical emergencies, a fact for which I am very grateful. I did have to deliver the prescribed medications during my shift, and if any of the residents became out of control, which was referred to as "going on the buck," I had to call the duty doctor and get permission to administer a shot, usually valium. I had to draw it up into the needle, and give the shot. Previous to this the only shots I had given were to oranges, and that was with supervision. It was very scary, but I needed a job so I did what I had to do.

 When I wasn't giving prescribed meds I worked directly with the residents on one of the wards, as a therapy aide. The building I worked in contained adult retarded women of different ages and different degrees of retardation. Most of these women had grown up in institutions and were products of a system where the higher functioning women took care of the lower functioning women. They fed them, dressed them and lead them around. I don't think they had separate rooms in the

---

  improve community placement for the now designated "Willowbrook class".

past. They just shared a large open room with rows of single beds.

The wards in the building where I worked consisted of a large common room we called the day room, from that in one direction a hall with rooms on either side, and the other side opened to the the elevator and the area where food was distributed between the two wings. During the night our job was just to see that things ran smoothly, and everyone stayed in their beds. We attempted to de-escalate situations by talking first, then gentle restraint. For major problems during the week we would call the RN. On weekends, I would be called to give a prescribed shot. It could be very dangerous; some of these women were very strong. I can remember one woman getting very agitated and pulling sinks away from the wall and trying to throw them at us. A lot of the women didn't have verbal skills, and had been in institutions most of their lives. When they threw temper tantrums, things could escalate very quickly. We were able to subdue the woman pulling the sinks and a shot was given, she calmed down, it was all part of another night at work.

In the morning our job was to get the residents up, and teach them to dress themselves. To understand the futility of this you need to remember that these women were already adults with patterns set. Previously the women, who could dress themselves, would do so, and then dress other women, many times they had their favorite friends that they wanted to take care of. We came along and upset their way of life, which didn't always go over very well. Most of us didn't have any training in teaching retarded adults how to do things. The truth is that not much teaching went on. We had about an hour to see that 25 residents were dressed and ready for breakfast each morning. Since there were two or three of us, just getting them ready was quite a challenge. The staffing was two therapy aids on each wing, with a floater to go to which ever side she was needed on.

As an example, there was a resident named Sharon, she liked to dress herself. After she was dressed she would be sent to join the other residents in the day room. As we got other residents dressed we would send them into the day room to wait for breakfast. Sometimes we could not spare a worker to supervise those waiting in the day room. Sharon liked to dress herself very much, and she didn't seem to understand that she was only supposed to wear one set of clothes at time. She would undress other residents and put their clothes on. It wasn't rare to think everyone was ready for breakfast only to walk back into the day room, and find several naked residents sitting or walking around, and Sharon wearing their clothes. We would then have to get Sharon to give up the clothes she had stolen, and re-dress the other residents. One time as I was attempting to get some of the clothes off of Sharon she bit me on the shoulder. Since she didn't have any way to communicate except violently, it was a very dangerous situation.

Sometimes I was called on to work into the day shift if no one showed up to work. We would take a group of residents for a walk outside which was a very new experience for some of them. It was quite a challenge to keep them from eating the interesting things they found on the ground.

I continued working at this job until spring 1978, when I accepted a position at IBM.

The Willowbrook Decree was a very good and important thing, but without proper staffing, it was slow to see results. It did bring sunlight into a very dark and gloomy system, and improve the lives of many.

Pat's IBM

Since my job at the Harlem Valley Psychiatric Center was really pretty awful and there wasn't any chance of advancement. I followed the suggestion of a friend by applying for a job at IBM in East Fishkill, New York. About six weeks after I applied at IBM, I received the letter telling me that I was offered a position. I accepted it and started work March 1978. I started in the T1 Pilot line which was a microchip development facility. I worked mostly second shift while I worked there. Later in 1978 I was transferred to the FET (Field-Effect Transistor) line, a chip production area but the processes were not still in development as they had been on the T1 Pilot line.

Since even a tiny bit of dust or hair could ruin the tiny circuits on the microchips the area I was working in was a "clean area." We had to wear white jump suits, with hoods that covered our hair, and booties to cover our shoes. The microchips were made by printing blocks of circuits on large wafers made of silicon. The wafers were about 4 inches in diameter, and would be cut into many little squares that would become the microchips for computers after they were completed.

Some of the processes used very harsh chemicals like sulfuric and hydrofluoric acid to etch out the circuit lines. The chemicals came in gallon bottles and had to be poured into vats so that the silicon wafers could be submerged into them for specific amounts of time. I used to come to work two hours early each day to pour the chemicals and to earn extra money. Because these chemicals were so caustic when I worked with them, I had to wear special heavy rubber gloves, a large apron, and a plastic face shield hooked to a helmet.

During the time I worked in the Masterslice T1 and Masterslice areas I became proficient in the operation of many machines that were used in process and also in testing. The reason these are called Masterslice areas is because they were the foundation processes that were used to make chips at that time. As part of my job I sometimes ran a big machine called the "Silox Machine." For this process the silicon wafers would be placed on a track one after the other, and would go through a chamber where silicon oxide with different elements added would be deposited on the wafers as they slowly went through the chamber. There were a lot of particulates floating around the room, and the machine had to be vacuumed frequently. While I worked in this room I had to wear a special gas mask for protection from the particulates. Some of the gasses that were used were very combustible so there were alarms to warn of any problems with the exhaust. It was really pretty dangerous, but IBM followed all of the OSHA (US Department of Labor: Occupational Safety and Health Administration) regulations that were necessary to keep us all safe.

During the spring of 1983 to get out of the clean room, I went to the probe shop. This was a pretty nice job, I didn't have to wear the white jump suit or work with dangerous or lethal chemicals. I used a little brush with grain alcohol to clean the ends of the probes that went onto the testers that were used to test the circuits on the chips. Sometimes I would have to straighten or replace the little pins on the probes.

I worked there for about six months when I discovered that the alcohol fumes were bothering me. I contacted the medical department about my allergy to alcohol. Since at the time IBM was a company that cared and respected their employees, my manager was told by the medical department to transfer me to another area. As my good fortune would have it one of his hunting buddies had room for one more employee in his department. In 1984 I went to work for him in quality control. Good fortune came my way again since there was a new technician program starting and quality control was scheduled to send two people. I was new to the department and didn't have any responsibilities yet, therefore I was chosen as one of them.

The program consisted of six months of classes at Marist College in Poughkeepsie going to school full time. After that I attended class in the morning, worked as assistant to an engineer in the afternoon, and at night I had homework. The classes were mostly technical; math, chemistry and physics. After six months of classes and work I had six months of working with the engineer I was assigned to helping with experiments and day to day work. This is where I learned to use the manual elipsometer. The elipsometer is a measurement tool that measures very thin films by using the refraction of the light as it goes through the film and bounces off the surface below. It was one of the most precise measurement tools at the time. It may sound boring, but I actually did enjoy it, and it was a skill that not many people had perfected.

After completing this school and training, I was promoted within the quality control department to Inspection Technician. My duties on that job were to go into the clean room areas where chips were being produced and perform audits and record any incorrect procedures the tool operators performed or any mistakes they made, compile reports and track when the problems were corrected.

As time went by and technology progressed there were more reorganizations within the company at the East Fishkill site, I was placed in another department within quality control. I think that is when the name was changed to quality assurance. During 1989 while working for Paul Chaloux, since I completed required IBM classes I was promoted to Senior Quality Specialist.

I learned to write programs using SAS (Statistical Analysis System) software products. This allowed me to create reports, compile charts and graphs to better show the information that had been collected as the chips were being measured at different stages of development, so that trends could be recognized and corrective actions taken in a timely manner.

1992 Lou Gerstner took over as the CEO of IBM and the lay-offs, buy outs, and reorganizations started. Prior to this time working at IBM was a secure lifetime career. The quality assurance groups were going to be done away with, and I most likely would be without a job. Workers were needed at the Burlington, Vermont, plant and there was an opportunity to go up there and work for six months then retire with a pretty good package. Also the increase in pay due to the shift premium over the six months would increase retirement benefits since the retirement at that time was calculated on how much you earned during your employment. The jobs at Burlington were temporary assignments and we would get housing allowance, moving expenses, and extra shift premium since we would be working twelve hour days. It was a rotating kind of schedule so about every three weeks I would get four days off and I would come back home to Pleasant Valley.

I had only been there a couple of months when everything changed. We were told to either find jobs for ourselves or we would be laid off. I wasn't really in a position to lose my job and I didn't want to move to Burlington, even thought at that time IBM would help sell my house in Pleasant Valley and pay for my move to Burlington if I found a job there. I didn't want to leave Pleasant Valley, so I didn't start looking for a job in Burlington.

Before my job was over in Burlington, I was contacted by an Engineer who I used to work with in East Fishkill asking if I was interested there working as his technician. The Siemens Corporation of Germany had signed a contract with IBM and insisted that IBM provide a quality engineer and technician. Because I was familiar with the processes and systems, he wondered if I would be interested in the job. The job was open to anyone within IBM. I applied, was interviewed, and got the job because of my experience. This extended my IBM career several more years. I enjoyed working with the Siemens Management and learned a lot of organizational skills from them. It was during this time in 1997 that I was promoted from Technical Laboratory Specialist to Senior Laboratory Specialist. While I reported to a Siemens manager, I also reported to IBM managers. They gave me raises according to the feedback they got from my Siemens manager, and I continued this phase of me employment until 2000.

More reorganizations and lay offs happened and in 2000 I was transferred within IBM to another job still at East Fishkill in the Analytical Services Operations Department keeping track of misprocessed, broken, or lost silicon wafers. As part of this job, I was in charge of something we referred to as "Scrap Court". When there was a loss of 5 or more of these silicon wafers for any reason I would investigate and assign blame. Sometimes it was a tool malfunctioning, engineer in charge of the tool would present the cause and corrective action. If it was a manufacturing employee, his manager would have to go to the meeting. The person who was assigned the blame had to go to a meeting of upper management and explain what went wrong and what he or she would do so that it never happened again. I then had to keep track that the actions really worked. I was also responsible for tracking process yields. I created and maintained data systems that were used to accomplish this.

June 4, 2002, was the day for layoff notifications to be made. I was selected for permanent layoff. Each person was called to his manager's office and told he still had a job or was informed that he was selected for permanent lay off, and would be given a "package." The package that I received was 6 months pay, opportunity to take classes and use computers to search for jobs at a special placement/training office that was set up for us, $2500 reimbursement for any school I chose, and retirement income when I reached 62 years of age. That part wasn't very bad for me since I was 62 already. I was given time off with pay and during that time I could look for a job within IBM. On July 9, 2002, I would come back and sign my papers, get my check and go on vacation then back home and to school. I used the school time to learn more about photography and to also give myself some structure in my life since it is quite an adjustment to all of a sudden not have a job after over 40 years of having one, or many as in my case.

I am grateful for everything I learned at IBM. I am most grateful that I worked for IBM during a time when they provided retirement income and health insurance to retirees. It has provided me with a happy and fun retirement.

Pat's Coffee Break

    The year was 1993 and it was becoming apparent that my regular job at IBM was not as stable as I had always thought it would be. There had been a very real threat of my being laid off, and I decided that I would need a back-up job. I liked coffee so it seemed to me a good idea to open a coffee shop. The name would be "Pat's Coffee Break." I found a local coffee roaster and started learning about and purchasing coffee. A friend who was a graphic artist helped me create a logo. I had clear labels printed with black writing and ordered white coffee bags to put labels on in two sizes one for half pounds the other for whole pounds.

    I started looking for a place to sell my coffee. I was friends with the man who was renting the store where my mother had been born. It had been my grandfather's store at the time. It was on the main street right in the middle of Pleasant Valley. He gave me space on a couple of shelves to display my bags of coffee, and he got a percentage of every bag that sold. This seemed to me to be a good omen: I was following in my grandfathers foot steps, I was sure I would be successful and build these few shelves into a prospering coffee shop. I just needed to find more space. The few bags of coffee I sold from that store didn't get me much profit, and the store wasn't doing much business either so the man who ran it retired. I decided if I was going to follow in my grandfather's foot steps I would have to do it some other place.

    During this time I didn't have a washing machine so every week I went to the local laundromat. One day I brought my coffee pot in and gave samples of my coffee to some of my friends who were there doing their laundry. I marked this as the official start of my business so it was soon after that I officially registered "Pat's Coffee Break" as a business name with the Dutchess county clerk's office.

I met with a SCORE Volunteer[5] to discuss a plan for my business. They directed me to Marist College where writing my business plan became a project for a group of business students. The students actually wrote the business plan for me using my input. While we were working on the business plan, I looked into a very nice location in Millbrook, New York, which had a dance studio attached. Since Millbrook was an affluent community it seemed to be a prime location. There were some celebrities who had summer or vacation homes there: Mary Tyler Moore, John Oats of Hall and Oats fame and several others. That location didn't work out, someone came forward with more money. They were able to rent the property sooner than I could.

I spoke with the the rental agent for a local mall, although the location that was available (very near one of the entrances) would have been very good, the rent there would be much too high for a starting business.

I also spoke with the owner of a small strip mall in Pleasant Valley, and was actually ready to sign papers to rent a small space next to an optometrist office. There was a dentist office upstairs over the space I looked at, but the dentist objected. His complaint was that I may be selling sweet items and the odor of sugar would not be good for his practice. He threatened to move if the space downstairs was rented to me, and since he had been a long time tenant and rented a large space he won, and I was unable to rent that space.

---

[5] SCORE "Counselors to America's Small Business" http://www.score.org

Since I couldn't find a space to rent, work on the business plan became just an exercise in learning about business plans. I decided that I would change my strategy and become a movable coffee business. My first attempt was at a local flea market in April 1994. I put up a table with a table cloth and since I didn't have electricity I brought two large silver insulated thermoses with hot coffee, some iced tea and bags of coffee. Although I did my best to sell, I didn't sell much, but I learned a valuable lesson. When people come to a flea market where items are displayed in rows on the ground they are looking for bargains not $1.00 cups or $8.00 pounds of coffee.

I decided that my best plan if I really wanted to have a coffee business was that I needed an altered business plan and more equipment. I looked into outdoor venues and purchased two more large silver thermoses. I would need one each for flavored and non-flavored coffee and also I would need to offer decaf or regular, so I purchased another table that could fold and fit on the floor of the back seat of my burgundy Honda Accord, and more table clothes to dress up the tables. I purchased a large blue banner with my logo and name, a large blue and white cooler for ice, glass gallon jugs for iced tea, some nice baskets for sugar and sweetener packets. My daughter Karen who has a tie dye business screen printed and tie dyed tee shirts and aprons and printed my logo on little white flags.

It was a time when local farm markets were starting to be organized, so when Pleasant Valley started a Farmers market, I joined. Every Friday I would take off from work at noon and go home to brew coffee and make tea for the market since there wasn't any electricity available there. Even after I put filter equipment on my household water supply the water still had sulfur in it which caused me to have to buy almost all of the water I used for coffee or tea. During the week I would grind and bag coffee so it would be ready for the market. I also sold bags of coffee to my friends during the week. I got a lot of help from my son, Tony, who was more experienced with retail sales since he worked at a deli and had been working there for quite sometime. He would have things ready for me when I arrived home on Fridays.

During 1994, besides selling at the farmers market on Friday afternoons, I set up and sold at every small festival I could fit in my schedule. Over time, I hired many of my friends to help me. My friend, Joanne, was a faithful helper; she spent many afternoons with me setting up and waiting for customers at various festivals around different towns. My cousin's daughter, Karina, was especially helpful because not only was she quick and good with the customers ,she could make the sign board where I listed the prices look clever and pleasing to the eye.

To do all of these outside venues I needed some shelter, so I purchased an "Easy-Up" that is a white canopy that is held by four tall posts and folds up to be about 2 feet by 2 feet wide and almost as long as a car is wide. It fit very nicely on the back seat of my car.

In May 1994, a friend from work was deciding to sell his pop-up camper so I went to look at it and had the idea that it could be converted into a coffee trailer. Since the trailers were very expensive, I bought the pop-up camper from him for $100. I got some estimates for the work that I wanted done to convert this camper to a mobile coffee stand. The estimate that I accepted to fix it up was from a carpenter named Bob. The estimate was that it would cost between $450 and $1000. In June 1994 I gave Bob $300, and delivered the trailer to his front yard, for work to be done. Although we didn't have a signed contract, I thought that I was very clear. I needed the job done as quickly as possible so that I could use it at a big festival in Kingston, New York, during the summer. I had to pay another $300 for Plexiglas that he needed for the sides. I should have realized that something was wrong then when he came upon such a large unexpected expense, or when I noticed that he had cut the tips of three of his fingers off. I just thought that meant he had been a carpenter for a long time. I didn't think that he could be clumsy or maybe inept.

During August 1994 it was apparent that the trailer wouldn't be ready for the summer, so I bought a van so I would have more room to carry all of my equipment.

By December 31, 1994, the trailer still wasn't fixed and I hadn't heard anything from Bob. I went with a couple of friends and picked up the trailer at Bob's house because the license plate on the trailer was going to expire and I wouldn't be able to pull it on the road. Also I wanted my trailer back. In January 1995 I got my first official bill from Bob for $1,746. I didn't pay the bill since the work hadn't been done, so Bob put a lien on my trailer. I had to hire a lawyer and go to court to get the lien off my trailer and to dispute the bill since we didn't have a written contract and I didn't believe I owed him as much as he claimed. I ended up paying Bob $432.80 ($350 plus $82.80 interest) plus I had to pay court cost of $20 and my lawyer $155.

My lawyer told me I could pay the debt off monthly, so I decided I would pay $50 per month. As soon as I paid my first $50, Bob's lawyer put a hold on all of my bank accounts including the accounts that belonged to my kids and were under my account number. I had to pay the entire amount before my money was released.

I gave the trailer to one of my son's friends and chalked the incident up as a learning experience. I will always have a signed contract and references before I hire a contractor.

I went to coffee seminars in Atlanta, Georgia, and Philadelphia, Pennsylvania, and even a coffee convention at the Javits Center in New York City. I learned how much better the coffee from Arabica beans is over the cheaper commercial brands with Robusta beans, and I became familiar with the plight of the poor children of the coffee pickers. I learned a lot about espresso, but due to the expense of the machine ($4000) and my limitations with electricity and water supply, I decided it wasn't for me.

During 1995 and 1996 a farmers market started at Baird Park, which is in New York, and along the Taconic Parkway, a main highway for people going to the country from New York City, and back on weekends. The park supervisor did a great job of publicity and had music every week. It became a weekly stop for travelers and locals alike. On sunny summer Sundays I would sell all of the iced tea I could bring, and all of the coffee I could make. I had to hire employees to help, which was good when we were busy, but when it rained, people didn't attend as much and the ones who did didn't buy very much to drink. Of course I would still have to pay my employees, that cancelled my profit from the good weekends. I continued at the Pleasant Valley markets on Fridays and on Saturdays I cleaned up from Friday or sold at whatever festival I could find. On Sundays I continued to rent space at Baird Park until the supervisor was transferred and the markets were discontinued. When Pleasant Valley had their 175th town celebration I rented a spot at the festivities and also had travel mugs for sale with my name and logo on. I still have some of those mugs, but not as many matching lids.

When I took a realistic look at the amount of energy, time and money I was putting into my coffee business, and the return I was getting, I decided that I was better off to put my energy into my job at IBM and it was time to have some fun when I wasn't at work instead of working all the time. I had learned a lot, but the coffee business wasn't for me. I sold my coffee pots and went on vacation.

Pat Holt

Merchandiser

I had just retired from IBM, and through pressure from a friend decided that I would apply for a job as a merchandiser. She said it was like shopping and we would go to different Stop' n Shop grocery stores. We would be part of a team that rearranged items on the shelves. That didn't seem too bad since we were going to get paid $10 an hour, and we would get paid for mileage. I don't really like to shop very much, but I figured if I was getting paid it would be ok.

The job was three days a week, Monday, Tuesday, and Wednesday from 8 AM to 3:30 PM, and we got 30 minutes for lunch and a break in the morning. I could work all three days or just one or two, however it fit into my schedule. We worked in six different Stop' n Shop grocery stores. Two were in Connecticut, and the other four were in New York State. We didn't get paid for the first 25 miles, but did get 25 cents a mile for every mile after that. Since only the stores in Connecticut and one of the New York stores were over 25 miles round trip. I found I only got paid for part of the mileage to travel to them.

It started out as a pretty good job, even if we did have a dress code which was no jeans or sneakers. This rule caused me to have to buy some new slacks and shoes. There were usually six of us, most of us worked for different merchandising companies. We had a Team Leader whose name was Bill. He made sure that we knew what we were supposed to do and he interfaced with the store management. He assigned us our jobs within our team. Bill, like most of the other employees had worked in the grocery business for many years and was retired from his regular job.

The first company I worked for insisted that I call the main 800 number every morning so they would know that I was at the store and had reported for work. At some point during my short employment another company bought them out, so I didn't have to call in any more.

Our main job was to rearrange items on the shelves of the various stores that we were assigned to according to the planogram. A planogram defines which product is placed in which area of a shelving unit and with which quantity, usually in order to increase customer purchases. These plans came from the main office at the store headquarters. I always wondered who changed the grocery store shelf layouts, now I know because it was my job: I was one of them. Sometimes products are moved to increase the sale of one product over another. We all thought that there was graft or lobbying to accomplish this. Other times it was due to the fact that a product had been discontinued by the company or the store had chosen not to carry some items. One time we had to move all of the high quality olive oils out of a store and replace them with some cheaper generic brands. I felt bad for the customers of that store because it was located close to Poughkeepsie, and it was on the bus route for the people who couldn't afford cars. I guess they figured that their demographic was poor people, and poor people don't want high quality olive oil.

I actually enjoyed the work, and the other workers were friendly. I tried not to think about the customers that couldn't find the soup, broth or olive oil they were looking for because we had moved it around or taken it away altogether. Also when we moved the products, we culled the out of date items and dusted the shelves which was a nice bonus for the shoppers. I did so well that I was promoted or I guess that's what it was.

I was assigned to go with one of the other women and learn about cutting in new products, this worked out well when she was with me, but as time went by I was expected to do this job by myself. Bill and everyone else on the team seemed to be familiar with the layout of the stores. I, like most of the shoppers, was pretty much lost as I wandered around the store looking for the items I was supposed to find. To my teammates it all seemed to be so simple, but to me it was like an ever-changing maze with no rhyme or reason to where things were placed.

    To cut in new products I would get several sheets of paper with various new products listed, like a new scent of dish detergent. Then I would have to find that product and see if the new item was already on the shelf. If it was not already on the shelf, I would have to make a space for it, and mark it so a tag could be made. If it was there, I indicated that on my sheet of paper and went on to the next item. Of course along with these new items there were the discontinued items, the ones that have become a favorite. For some unknown reason that product was longer available. When I came across these items, we would remove them from the shelf, remove the tag and write it on our paper. Those items would be taken to the store room. Then near the end of the day our team leader would give me new shelf tags and I would have to go around finding all of the places that they belonged and put them on the shelves. This was way too much like shopping, and I didn't like it at all.

I kept working on and off for two years. As my busy life kept getting in the way of my working, I worked less and less until I quit all together. I stopped having time to work.

Pat Holt

My Summer Job

It was summer 2007, my first full summer in Columbia, Missouri. I was thinking about the fact that I really needed more money. *I guess I'll look for a job in the Columbia Tribune* I thought.

As I sat in my favorite brown chair looking at the want ads, *there it is!* "**Deliver Telephone Books**." I quickly called the 800 number listed in the ad, thinking *I better hurry before someone else gets the job*. It seemed to be just the job for me. I could set my own hours, take my time, and get some extra money. A recorded message told me to leave my name and phone number and that my call would be returned shortly. The call finally came after what seemed like a very long wait. I was told to come to the Days Inn on I-70 outer road at 1:30 PM on Thursday, June 15, for an interview.

When I arrived at the Days Inn and drove around to the back where the room I was told to go to was located for what I expected to be an interview, I couldn't help but notice there were several people already waiting, and a bustle of activity. It all seemed quite curious to me as I took my place at the end of a short line of potential employees. When it came to my turn I was given papers to fill out about my name, age and social security number, the young girl accepting the paperwork said to me, "I will need to make a copy of your driver's license and your auto insurance card." The driver's license wasn't a problem, but I couldn't find my insurance card. She didn't believe I had insurance, or else she just needed a copy of the card to complete the paperwork. No problem for me, the soon-to-be-employee of the telephone book distribution company.

My insurance agent's office was less than a mile from where we were, so I could just go over there and pick up a copy of my insurance card. I drove the 5 blocks to my insurance agent's office, and was quickly given a copy of my insurance card. After I returned with my proof of insurance so a copy could be made I was hired immediately and was offered a choice of several routes, some inside the city limits and some outside in rural towns. I could choose the route that I wanted. I thought that in the city limits would be best for me, since I was familiar with most of the city. I could choose a route on and around the campus that looked very confusing to me or a section of the city that I was familiar with along Garth where my grandkids went to school. That seemed to be a good choice to me at the time. There were large trees along the street to provide shade from the hot June sun, and the houses were close together. A nice quiet residential area. It seemed like a pretty big route, but it did include a couple of big office buildings, which seemed to me, would be easy, all air conditioned and cool. There were a couple of apartment buildings, and a doctor's park which seemed to me, since they were close together, should go fast.

  Of course it was a lot of books to deliver, 667 big books, and 536 small books, and at least 600 plastic bags for when the customer needed one big and one small book. The "big" telephone books were a little over 1 ½ inch thick and the "small" telephone books were about ½ inch thick. The big books were the normal phone books that contain both white pages and yellow pages, but the smaller books are the idea of someone who never delivered telephone books, or thought about wasting paper. These contained only yellow pages, and were pretty much a waste of resources.

  I had to watch a short film about where to leave the phone books. The bag with books must go on the hinge side of the door, and should lean against the hinge, not lay down flat on the porch. Of course this meant that I must walk up each sidewalk, and onto every porch to place the phone book carefully at the hinge side of the door. We were told that random calls would be made to people along the routes to check that we did our jobs properly. There would also be people scattered throughout the list that had to sign that they received a phone book. These all seemed to be people who advertised in the yellow pages, so they had offices, and hopefully would be easy to find. The list also contained codes for who should get the standard two book package of one big and one small book, and who should get two big books and one small book. It seems that if you have two telephones, you get a big phone book for each phone.

  I was almost ready for phase two, getting the phone books home so I could bag them and start my delivery, which I found was supposed to be complete by Monday afternoon. I was given approximately 600 plastic bags, and sent to get in line to have my car loaded with telephone books.

  The day was pretty hot, and there wasn't much shade in the Days Inn parking lot. As I waited my turn I spent the time chatting with a couple of the people that were ahead of me. Finally it was my turn, I backed up to the trailer and gave my paperwork to one of the men. He told the workers what I needed and they loaded 240 big books, and 240 small books into my car. As I was driving home I noticed that it was almost 4:00 on Friday afternoon, and I still had over 400 more big books, and almost 200 small books left to get home. I began to think about the reality of what I had signed up to do, and grew a little nervous. I never realized how large a pile of phone books could be, or how heavy. I got home with my first load, and my car was riding pretty low with that entire wait. I unloaded my car, and piled the phone books in my living room. I couldn't go back to get more books Friday night, since the workers had stopped for the night. I called my daughter, Karen and explained my dilemma. She said she would help by putting the books into bags while I went to get more on Saturday morning. Saturday morning I was at the parking lot by 7:30 and got in line to have my car loaded. At 8:00 the workers came and started loading cars. After about and hour wait I got my car loaded again, and headed home to unload and come back for more. I found that it took about three totally full Toyota Camry loads to get 667 big phone books and 536 small phone books from the trailers to my house.

By the time I was home and ready to start delivering the books it was almost noon on Saturday. Karen had bagged non-stop while I was transporting the books to my house. She did stop to help me unload my car when I got home from my pick-up trips. I had a quick bite to eat, loaded my little cooler with ice and bottles of water, and together we loaded my car. To transport the bags of books to my car and beyond, she had filled every milk crate and large plastic tub that I owned since they were no longer bundled together but were in slippery plastic bags. I had decided that the small dolly that I used to move heavy objects would be the perfect transportation device. It didn't take up much room, and it would help me carry several milk crates full of books at one time.

The temperature was over 95 degrees, but I was undaunted as I headed out on my new adventure. I still thought that the shade from the trees that lined the residential streets would provide refuge from the heat, so my first destination would somehow be cool. I found a parking place a ways up the street, so I could deliver down to the end of Garth and up about an equal distance. I carefully loaded up my dolly with boxes of phone books, and with my list in hand, I started off. I hadn't gone very far up and down walkways, up and down porch steps when I discovered that when it is over 95 degrees it is hot even when you are in the shade.

After I finished delivering on Garth, I went into the library to use the restroom and get a little cooled off. I went back to delivering on several nearby streets until my car was emptied.

By the time I got home Saturday evening I was exhausted, my feet hurt, and I was hungry, Karen could hardly lift her hands from the repetition of putting books in bags all day. I decided to take her and her family out to dinner since neither of us had the energy to cook, and she didn't think she could hold a pot or pan.

I planned to start again early Sunday morning, and Karen came over to finish bagging books. We loaded my car and I was determined to finish as many residential deliveries as I could get to. I finished Garth on the other side of Broadway, West Ash, McBain, and on and on. As the sun was beginning to set I was totally worn out. I had been up and down too many stairs and in and out of too many hot apartment buildings. I didn't realize that apartment buildings didn't cool the halls and stairways. Between apartment buildings I would sit in my car with the air conditioning on so that I could cool off.

Sunday night I took us all out to dinner again because Karen and I were too tired, and her wrists were still tired and sore. I had one day left to finish what I had thought in the beginning would be an easy job.

Monday morning I started out ready to distribute phone books to the offices which I thought would go quickly. I went into the first office building to check it out. The office names were on the doors, *this will be easy*, I thought. I went back to my car, brought in as many books as I could manage, placed them in a corner of the lobby and checked my list. The names on my list didn't match the reality of what was listed by the doors. I needed a lot of signatures from people in the building so I had to find the correct people. It took hours, most of the morning in fact, but I succeeded. The next office building was much easier since the people hadn't moved around as much. Back home to re-load my car and then all that remained was the Doctors' Park which seemed pretty straight forward; five buildings each marked somewhat clearly and there were name plaques by almost every door. Several of these people had moved within the park or left entirely but hadn't bothered to take their name plaques with them. This became as time consuming and complex as the first office building I had entered. I got the books delivered and either got the signatures I needed and listed the new office addresses within the park or indicated "moved" where people had moved away. By sunset Monday I had delivered or accounted for all but a few book deliveries. The phone book distribution office was closed for the day. I finished my paperwork so I would be ready to get this job behind me Tuesday morning. I planned to once again start early and finish the few deliveries Tuesday morning, so I could be at the Days Inn office when they opened to turn in my paperwork and return the few undelivered books.

    I made it! Since I had successfully delivered all of my books and completed my paperwork so efficiently, I was given the $30 bonus as if I had completed Monday evening instead of Tuesday morning.

    I ended up getting a check for $255 which included $30 for car allowance. When I look at my expenses, it cost me about $300 for meals and gas not even considering the wear and tear on my daughter and me and my car.

    The following summer I got a call from the phone book distribution company inquiring if I would like to deliver phone books again. I turned down the job, this is not a job I would sign-up to do again.

Cats In My Life

There have been many cats in my life, in spite of the fact that I am not a cat person.

This summer when I went back to Pleasant Valley to visit, I needed a place to stay, and it just happened that a dear friend was going to be away. She said I could stay at her house while she was away if I wanted, and in return all I had to do was feed her cats and let them in and out. That sounded like a very good deal to me. She has three cats: Missy is grey: Sasha is a brown tabby, and NC, which is short for North Carolina is orange.

The nice things about these cats are that they didn't jump up onto tables, counters or beds. They also didn't use the littler box. By that I mean they always went to the bathroom outside. They spent about half the time outside and half inside.

This is how our day went. In the morning whoever was inside the house happily ate the dry and canned food I provided and drank the fresh water, and sometimes I would add a treat or two. After breakfast they might lie around a little while, but usually at least one would go to the front door (always the front door). After I let him out and sat back down to my own breakfast, another would want to come in or go out. The way they would let me know they wanted to go out was to pull on the loose weather stripping at the bottom of the door with a paw and cause it to snap loudly. When they wanted me to let them in, they would sit on the air conditioner outside the window nearest the front door and pick at the screen.

When Sasha was in the house, she would usually curl up cat fashion in a nice high back chair in a corner of the dining room, or when I was on the couch she moved to a cushion in the center of the couch. When I moved the cushion to the side so that I could have more room, she would not sleep on the cushion, but still in the center of the couch. NC had her own chair in the living room, Missy mostly slept on the screened-in back porch. It was very normal in the middle of the night to wake up to the ""Bang, bang" of the door so that I would know to let a cat out. I would get back in bed. As I settled myself, the "Plunk, plunk" of the screen would signify it was time someone wanted to come in. When I would open the door to let in one of them, it sometimes crossed my mind *"I hope some strange animal doesn't follow them in!"* I know that sometimes raccoons do enter houses at night if there is food and they get the chance. Fortunately during the night that never happened, it was only the friendly house cats that came in when I opened the door.

During the last morning of my stay, while I was frying bacon for my breakfast, a cat that I thought was Sasha looked in the kitchen window. This was very strange since she had always come and gone through the front door. I imagined she had smelled the bacon frying and was looking in to see what was going on. As I let her in the kitchen door, I told her it was strange for her to come in that door, but I bet it smelled good in here. She no more got into the kitchen than she sprung up onto the stove top! Lucky for all of us, it wasn't a gas stove with a flame. It was the kind of electric stove that has a flat surface with the heating coils imbedded in it. As she hit the stove top, the pan slid and so did she. I grabbed the pan, and quickly pushed her to the floor. My first thought was *"This isn't Sasha!"* To escape the kitchen she ran toward the living room, with me right behind her, when I cornered her at the door, she hissed at me, I opened the door and whisked her out. I will never know if it was Sasha overcome by the enticing smell of bacon frying or some strange neighborhood cat that I let in by mistake. Which ever it was I got her out before any damage was done, and I saved my bacon.

Back home in Columbia, when my friend Sue goes on vacation with her husband, I go look after and feed their cats while they are away. I did this last year, and it's not much bother. She lives less than a mile away, and I can fit it into my schedule whenever I want. Last year they had a cat door available so that sisters Kate, Molly, Tina, and big brother Teager II (spelled TEAGER) could come in, get food, and hang out in the house when they wanted. Kate is all orange, Molly is orange and white, Tina is beige and white, and Teager II is black and white. I don't know why they spell Tigger the way they do, I must remember to ask. There is also Ebony, the 20 year old black cat who is deaf. She has her own room but she can't go in and out like the others because of her deafness. Normally she does go up and down stairs and spend time where the family is, but when everyone is gone she has a special room all to herself. When Sue and her husband left for their one week vacation last year, I mentioned that leaving the cat door available in an empty house was a dangerous thing because some strange animal might get in. They said they had done it before with out a problem. I just needed to come over once a day and see that the cats had food and water and the litter was clean. For Ebony it was a little more, since she also needed wet food warmed a little, and the area around her litter box needed to be cleaned, since she didn't always get all the way into it and sometimes peed on the tray outside the box.

Everything went smoothly for the first six days, but on the seventh when I went upstairs with Ebony's food I noticed that her door was open. I wondered if I had left it open by mistake. She didn't wander off, so no harm done. I would just be more sure to close it. When I went to check the food for the other cats, it seemed they had eaten more than normal. I guessed being without their human family made them hungrier. The next day when Sue and her husband got home they found that a raccoon had gotten in the cat door, and made a very big mess. I'm glad it waited until my duties were finished to invade the home.

  This year once again I am on cat care duty for Sue, but this year there is no cat door, so no fear of hungry wild animals. Also two of us share the load, each having the responsibility for four days. Ebony's food doesn't have to be heated, but each day there is a pad so a little report can be made of Ebony's bowel and urinary output and also who comes in and who goes out, or who we don't see. Cat care went smoothly without any emergencies.

This is Pumpkin

  As I look back, I did have a cat of my own for a while. There were some feral cats living in my back yard that I used to trap and take to the SPCA to get fixed. When I missed one, there was a litter of kittens. One of them, she was grey and white with a little splotch of orange on her face, was limping, so I took her to the local veterinarian. After an x-ray he said she had broken the little ball on her hip that fits into the socket. I could choose to ignore it and let her limp for the rest of her life, because it would probably heal by itself, or for $350 he would operate. When I took her home she would have to stay in her cat cage, and slowly be allowed out for longer periods of time until she was completely mobile. I chose the option of the $350 fix. Once I did that, I named her Pumpkin and she had to become a house cat, because she was too valuable to be allowed outside where she might be hit by a car on the busy road that ran in front of our house. When I sold my house my son found a good home for her.

Now I am living in Columbia and still don't want the responsibility of a cat of my own, but when friends need cat care, I will be available.

Pat Holt

The Price of Ice Cream

As I was at the grocery store selecting which half gallon of ice cream I would buy, a friendly voice said, "Hi!". It was my daughter's neighbor, Susan. As we started talking, she let me in on the fact that I was looking at a container, which was a name brand with no unpronounceable additives, wasn't really a half gallon anymore, but was now 1.5 quarts. The store brand was 1.75 quarts, a little better deal. I was shocked!

This made me think of the ice cream cones we used to get when I was young in Pleasant Valley. There was a store that sold huge ice cream cones. It looked like almost a pint of ice cream on one cone. The cost was seven cents. My cousins Ronnie and Babs and I would walk down to the store, which was about a quarter mile from their house. We didn't wear shoes, even though the sidewalks were hot on our bare feet. We would get our ice cream cones and then we would race to see who could eat theirs quickest on the way back home. I never won!

My father had a cousin Ray who owned a gas station several miles away with a little store attached. The only time I ever remember going to visit him, I wanted an ice cream cone and my father had to pay for it. What was worse than him having to pay, was the fact that it cost ten cents, and had less ice cream than the ones we had gotten in Pleasant Valley, at the store where we didn't have a relative.

Last night as I was fixing myself a dish of ice cream I noticed how small my ice cream scoop was. *I guess that will make my expensive ice cream last longer,* I thought, trying to put a positive spin on my new obsession with the rising cost of ice cream.

Today I paid $1.40 for a small one scoop ice cream cone. I wonder how expensive ice cream can become?

My first house in 1985.

My First House

In the winter of 1979, the house I was renting with my two children was being sold and we needed a new place to live. A long-time family friend, Annie Davis had just frozen to death in her living room while her husband was in the hospital recovering from a heart attack. I had lived in Pleasant Valley most all of my life, and had known Annie since I was a child and her husband since they'd been married.

My Aunt Toddy, who lived across the street from Annie, was at her house during the evening to keep her company while Annie's husband was in the hospital because of some heart problems. The story, as Aunt Toddy told it, was that the furnace was not working so Annie was keeping warm by a wood stove in the living room. They had been having a few drinks, and as she was getting ready to leave, my aunt said she reminded Annie to stoke the wood fire because it was going to get very cold that night. Annie's reply was "Don't worry about it, have another drink." My aunt went home. When she went back to check on Annie the next morning, she found her frozen to death near her chair in the living room. The temperature had dropped to 20 below zero during the night, the fire had gone out, and everything in the house froze. The hospital released Annie's husband Warner for the funeral and to bury his wife.

After the funeral, as I was expressing my condolences to Warner, I asked him, "What are you going to do now?" "I'm going to go to Florida," he replied so I asked him if I could rent his house, since I needed a place to live. His answer was "I'll sell you the damn thing!"

At the time I was a single mother with two children: my son Tony almost 12 and my daughter Karen who had just turned 14. Although I wasn't getting child support, I had a good job at

IBM. We needed a place to live, so I decided to buy Warner's house.

After a few days, I went to see Warner to discuss the deal. The price decided on was $8,700. It was hard to find a place to get a mortgage for such a small amount even in 1979. I was able to get a mortgage for $6,000 from the IBM Credit Union and Warner held a note for $2,700 to cover the rest. The day we went to the lawyer to sign the papers for me to purchase the house Warner and I stopped at Kentucky Fried Chicken to have lunch on the way home and to celebrate signing the deal.

Warner headed south to Florida to get new teeth, and he was to return to clear out his house for me to close and take possession. A few days after he returned, he died suddenly. Since he had signed papers with me and the price had been agreed to, that deal was set. His sister agreed to it, and I signed the papers to take ownership of the house as soon as it was cleaned out.

Warner had worked at the local trash compactor where the residents brought their trash. He brought home everything he thought he might ever be able to use, so there was a lot to be removed. Warner's sister hired my cousin Ronnie to clean out the house. It took about a month to get it emptied enough for us to move in. While we were waiting to move in I looked in the county records and found that the house was most likely built in about 1849.

When I finally took ownership in May the sight was overwhelming. I wondered what I had gotten myself into! As I entered the house from the side door into the kitchen, extension cords snaked from one outlet to three different long florescent lights hanging from the ceiling. There were lights over the sink and stove, and another in the middle of the room. There was a hole in the wall over the stove which contained an exhaust fan that drew any fumes or smoke directly outside. The linoleum floor sagged due to the old beams rotting away in the cellar. All the ceilings were low, only six feet six inches tall, and at the door jams they were about 6 feet two inches. Unlike other houses with a space between the door jam and the ceiling, there was no room for a space here. This wasn't a problem for us since I was five feet seven inches, and my kids were of course shorter. The kitchen cabinets and walls were painted a light green that had grown dingy over the years. The cabinets seemed to be remodeled from store cabinets with drawers and a counter top covered with linoleum. To the immediate right was the doorway to the living room. You could see that the embossed tin ceiling was in good condition, but the walls were covered with cheap, simulated wood paneling, and the floor was covered with a dark green carpet. Straight ahead in the living room was the stove Annie had failed to keep going. It wasn't a store bought stove, but a jury-rigged job by Warner. It had been a metal water tank that had been laid on its side and legs had been attached. There was a door on hinges welded to the flat end, and part of the top had been cut away with a flat piece of steel welded there to make a flat surface for placing a pot of water to provide humidity. Near the rounded end of the tank a hole had been made for the stove pipe which extended to the chimney that also carried the smoke or fumes from the oil furnace that was in the cellar right underneath. This all sat on a large piece of metal that looked like a giant oval griddle. In the ceiling above the stove was a vent hole with a grill that allowed warm air to rise upwards into the bedroom. The living room had a bay window with three windows that looked out toward the road which ran too close to the front of the house. The top half of the front door was glass and the door knob was about knee height. It looked like a normal size door with the bottom cut off to make it fit.

A small room off the living room would have been referred to as the front parlor in the days back when the house was built. This room also had an embossed tin ceiling but not in as good a condition as the living room ceiling. The paint was peeling off and the plaster on the walls was cracking. The corners of this room were not square; the outside corner was less than a right angle since the house followed the property line which narrowed as it went away from the road and toward the creek. A door from this room led to a small, narrow hallway with a small anteroom at the bottom of the stairs from which you could also re-enter the kitchen. From the anteroom, the bathroom was on your left and the stairs to the bedrooms on the right. There was also a small closet. The bathroom contained a tub, toilet and sink. The sink was free standing. There were no countertops but pieces of thin copper pipe attached to the floor and supported the sink. The bathroom was very narrow; just enough room to walk in and sit on the toilet or stand at the sink, which actually became handy if anyone was sick.

The stairs were narrow and had a landing with a tight turn. To get our beds and dressers upstairs we had to put them through a large window in one of the bedrooms, which worked pretty well. We just removed the window parts, backed the truck up under the window, and handed items in to the person standing inside. We were all happy to see that the upstairs ceilings were one foot higher than the downstairs ceilings.

I chose the largest bedroom, the only one with a closet. It was at the front of the house, directly over the living room. The ceiling in my bedroom, like the ones downstairs was embossed tin. The walls were cracked plaster painted the same dingy green as the kitchen. The linoleum on the floor was multicolored with light-grey feather-like designs covering the wide board floor.

Tony took the smaller front bedroom. Although it was smaller with no closet, its condition was pretty much the same as mine.

Karen took the room over the kitchen, the room with the big window. There were times that she used that big window to leave the house and go with her friends when I told her to stay home. Her room was long and narrow and not as big as the kitchen. Her walls were made of some kind of old fashion wall board that was thick and textured, and part of her ceiling slanted toward the floor. Her floor was bare plywood.

At some point after Warner had bought the house he had added on most of what were the current kitchen and the upstairs room, now Karen's which is why it didn't match anything in the rest of the house.

A screened porch off the kitchen was really in pretty good shape. From it you could go out a door and over a little walkway to the garage. Most of the walls were screens and Warner had created an interesting way to close the porch in during the winter or stormy weather. The screens had long sills with smaller boards attached at the top and bottom forming a trough. He had glass shelves that he salvaged from an old drug store, which fit vertically in the trough and overlapped to keep out the wind and rain or snow. Over time the size of the trough had become larger requiring folded pieces of newspaper to be poked into the spaces between the pieces of glass to keep them from rattling in the wind.

The garage located over the little walkway and to the side of the house was not usable for a car; it was only good for storage since the footings had been damaged in a flood. The house was built on the hillside, as it dropped down toward the creek. There was space under the garage for a basement to be built, and another building attached to that on the side toward the creek. It was that building which my kids, mostly Karen, used as a place to hang out and have parties with their friends. Eventually, I grew upset with their behavior and tore it down.

Over the years as the road widened for more traffic, bringing it very close to the house, the bay window on the first floor ended up about 3 feet from the edge of the paved part of the road. There was a telephone pole between the house and the road on the northeast corner, providing a barrier for safety from cars that might slide off the road in bad weather.

As I said Warner used things he found. At one time he worked for the county highway department where he got the yellow paint that the road stripes are painted with and painted the whole outside of the house what we called "state road yellow." Fortunately the little glass beads don't go into the paint until after it is on, so the house didn't glow. Of course he trimmed it in "state road white."

The outside of the chimney looked impressive. Different sized fields stones had been cemented together with glass bricks imbedded in the front. Lights had been placed inside the wall. These lights worked at one time, I'm sure, but due to poor planning there was no way to change the bulbs without taking the glass brick out, and I didn't know how to do that. The chimney was 7 or 8 feet wide at the base. At a height of about 5 feet it tapered to a more normal chimney size. To accomplish this large pieces of slate covered the slope as the structure narrowed. On the side of the chimney near the kitchen door there was a milk box, attached with metal brackets. It may have been used long ago when a milkman delivered milk which he'd put into these metal insulated boxes if no one was home. I don't know if Warner ever had milk delivered that way or he just thought it was a good idea to have the box there. I planted flowers in it, since by the time I bought the house there weren't any milkmen delivering milk.

When I took ownership of the house the water pipes had frozen, and there wasn't any water in the house. Before we could completely move in, I had to have a plumber come and re-plumb the house. Even the pipes that weren't broken were of no use. They were a patchwork of pieces of galvanized and copper pipes. For that job I hired a local plumber, so it went rather smoothly and quickly. This brings me to the water supply. Pleasant Valley doesn't have municipal water. Every house has its own well and septic system, so we depended solely on a well. The well for my house was a hand-dug hole in the cellar. Depending on the well was fine as long as my kids and I correctly spaced our showers, dish washing, and any other chores that needed water. Clothes had to be taken to the laundromat for washing, which would have to be fixed, but later.

It seemed there were a lot of broken windows so I learned to cut and replace the glass. While I was doing this I thought it would be a good idea to paint the trim around the windows a color other than the state road white, so I painted the trim maroon.

The reason the furnace had gone out the night Annie died was that the oil in the line from the tank outside and under the back porch had frozen, so no oil could flame the fire. Once the line thawed, that problem was solved and the furnace started again for a while. Even when it was working the furnace was not dependable. Oil was too expensive for me to buy enough to burn it consistently. It was several years before I had the furnace fixed and a regular supply of oil so that it worked dependably with a thermostat. During that time we used the wood stove in the living room to attempt to keep warm when the furnace wasn't working. The stove was inefficient, and there wasn't any insulation in the walls of the house, so no matter how hot the fire in the stove got, a few feet from the stove was not warm. I tried using a fan to blow the heat around but that didn't help much. I remember one time when it was really cold outside we stood around the stove warming first our front side then our back. I hung a curtain in the opening between the living room and the front parlor so the heat would stay in the living room. If we needed to go to the bathroom which was always very cold we put on coats as we left the living room. I placed a small electric heater in the bathroom to keep us and the water from freezing. At night sometimes I would put newspapers on top of my blankets for extra insulation. Each morning I would get up early to re-light the stove to take the chill off the house, because the fire always went out in the night.

There was a building in my back yard that I tore down and burned in the stove. I knew that it wasn't a good thing to burn even old boards in a stove but we needed the wood, not the building, and it sure did make a really hot fire. I knew it was important to clean the chimney so I found a square chimney brush and two pieces of long rope. For some reason there was a removable hatch in the roof of my house. I used to imagine that it was where the original owners would go to watch and shoot Indians, but the hole was handy for cleaning the chimney, so that is probably why it was there. The opening into the attic was in my room over my dresser. First I would stand on my dresser, and then climb up through the opening into the attic. From there I could open the roof hatch and get onto the roof where I would drop the rope that was tied onto the bottom of the brush down the chimney, leaving another piece of long rope on the roof. Next I would go back into the house, down the stairs all the way to the cellar. A hole at the bottom of the chimney allowed me to pull the rope that was dangling there from the brush. When the brush was all the way down, I would go back up the stairs, back onto my dresser, up into the attic, onto the roof, and pull the rope to bring the brush back up. I would repeat this several times, until I was tired, then the chimney would be clean and I could seal up the roof and close the attic opening.

The last winter that I used the stove I purchased a load of firewood from a local nursery. It was only half a cord because I didn't have enough money for more. There were large branches of poison ivy in among the pieces of wood. I used the poison ivy as kindling to start the fire, before I realized what it was. Fortunately, since the fire was in the stove, not outdoors, I didn't breathe the smoke, but I did get such a bad case of poison ivy that I had to go to the emergency room to get some cortisone pills and ointment and missed several days of work. I had poison ivy on my neck, face, chest and arms and couldn't stand to wear clothes; I mostly just lay around wrapped in a sheet until the blisters went down and the itching lessened. During this time Tony and his friends lovingly referred to me as the monster from upstairs.

Soon after this I met a man named Tad where I worked at IBM. We became friendly and used to go out after work with other friends and have a few drinks. His idea of a good date for a Friday night was happy hour at a nearby bar and then back to the cafeteria at IBM for clam chowder. I never took him up on his offer of clam chowder at the cafeteria.

Tad was in some ways like Warner, the former owner of my house. When he saw the problem I was having with my water supply he came up with a solution that was innovative. A piece of black plastic pipe extended from the cellar of my house underground to the creek in the back yard about 60 feet away. He put a sump pump in the creek at the end of the pipe, and in the cellar he continued the pipe to the edge of the well. Over the well he fashioned a system of weights using a beer bottle and a canning jar. When the water in the well went down to a certain point the canning jar would stop floating. The weight of the jar would raise the beer bottle which would turn the sump pump on to draw water from the creek. As the well filled, to the point that the canning jar started to float, the beer bottle would drop down, and the pump would turn off until it was triggered again by the canning jar.

    This solution worked for a short while, but by 1980, I faced the fact that I needed a real well drilled by a professional well driller. I called the local well driller. He was familiar with my yard, and didn't want to try to get down the hill behind my house or park too close to the road, so he made excuses as to why he couldn't drill the well. I called a second well driller who took the job. He arrived with his equipment and started drilling about 6 feet from the north side of my house back far enough from the road so that he could fit his truck. They drilled, and drilled. Finally at about 350 feet he hit water, the cost $2000. He said that the pump would have to go 300 feet into the well to be sure that I would always have water. This was very strange to me since there was a well in my cellar that was about 12 feet from the ground level, and there was almost always water oozing from the ground across the street from a natural spring. There wasn't anyway for me to know for sure, so I had to take his word for the situation. When a pump is 300 feet down in a well, the amount of electricity needed to run that pump is a lot. Actually my house had antiquated electrical service only two 30 amp fuses in a fuse box. To get the water out of my new well I would need a 200 amp service. Tad was very helpful, installing the new circuit breaker box, connecting the pump and at the same time correcting a few of the wiring problems in my house. The work he did was good enough to pass inspection by the electric company. Some of my daughter's friends helped dig the trench and connect the pipes to bring the new well water into the house. As I stood at my kitchen sink and turned on the water faucet to see the miracle of an unlimited supply of water from my new expensive well, I smelled rotting eggs. My new water had sulfur in it and smelled and tasted awful. There wasn't anything that could be done as this was "An act of God," the well driller said. It was several years before I could afford to get a filtration system to take some of the sulfur smell out of the water, but even with a filter system it never completely went away.

Since Tad was about to leave his wife, he needed a place to stay. At the same time I needed money to pay my property tax, so he gave me the money, about $600. In return, I told him he could move in with me. The more I thought about the idea, the worse I thought it was. Since I had used the money I couldn't give it back, so I told him I didn't have room for him and that I would pay him back at a later date. He said he would sleep in my cellar! I was surprised about that since my cellar had a dirt floor and two of the four walls were just rocks piled up. The pipes and wires in the ceiling were all exposed as were the big old beams. I didn't feel like I had a choice so I agreed to let him stay in my cellar. He brought over several large pieces of plastic, some used for walls and one for the floor. On his floor he added a piece of indoor-outdoor carpet. Then he brought in a cot to sleep on. I don't know how or where he kept his clothes. I used to fix supper for us all and as I did he would sit at the table and look at me with what I thought was adoration, but I later decided he was just spacing out. Each night after he moved in he would descend the narrow wooden steps to his plastic lined room in my cellar.

It was around this time that I decided to go to a Methodist church singles group as a way of meeting new people. The first meeting I went to I met a woman who had been a friend of mine about 15 or 20 years prior, when my husband was helping her with her horse. She had just divorced from her husband and we renewed our friendship of long ago. We all went to different house parties and dances together. As things moved along, she and Tad got friendlier and at some point she and I hatched a scheme to bring her and Tad together. She had a big house, two children and a kennel. She needed help, both financial and physical. She invited him to move into a room in her house in return for some help. This seemed good for everyone so he moved in with her. My house had a way of bringing people together.

    I had plenty of electricity and water and Tad out of my cellar. Next I needed to do something about the way the floors were sagging. Through a friend I met a guy named Chuck who was a contractor. He was interested in me and wanted me to be his mistress. I told him I wasn't interested but he didn't seem to hear me. I wanted him to work for me as a contractor, jacking up my sagging floors and putting new supports under them. As he worked I talked about paying him. He would just steer the conversation to wanting to take me to bed and have me be his mistress, and that I should at least have a cup of tea with him instead of drinking beer with my friends. Chuck jacked up of my floors and put supports where he had made adjustments, but since I did not agree to be his mistress or even go to bed with him he lost interest and stopped coming around. I never did pay him anything for work he did, and he never sent me a bill.

    Karen went on a cross-country trip with some friends, stopped to visit her father in Columbia, Missouri, and stayed there where she married, had children, and started a business.

    After the major repairs that made my house habitable I did a major project each year when I got my income tax refund. The next major repair was a new roof, the old roof was tin, and had been on the house for many years. New siding would be needed to get rid of the "state road yellow", and storm and screen windows and doors would be a worthwhile addition.

After gathering a few prices, I decided that a total package to cover all was a good idea. So my house got a new shingled roof. I chose the color to look the most like the color the tin had been. It seemed that vinyl siding was a good choice, which would look good and also provide some insulation since they put a layer of plastic and thin insulation between the original shingles and the new vinyl siding to close up the cracks. The frames around the windows and doors would be covered; storm and screen windows and doors would also be added. This was done during the summer of 1984 or 1985 and covered the roof hatch and the hole that had been in the kitchen to provide exhaust for the stove.

It wasn't until 1994 when I refinanced my mortgage that I purchased a new furnace so the house would be warm in the winter

Since the garage wasn't usable, I tore it down with help from my neighbor. My son, Tony and a friend built a deck in the back yard where the basement under the garage had been. He also started landscaping the front and back yards. Tony has the landscaper gene from my father and Aunt Donna, who were both gifted with the ability to put the correct flowers and shrubs together to make beautiful gardens, and to keep them looking that way. He made some really nice and well coordinated garden spots around the yard.

I had some more supports put under the kitchen and a new ceramic tile floor and new sink installed. A friend came over and helped me tear down the ceiling and cabinets so I could have them replaced. I am sorry I don't have pictures of what we took down from the ceiling. It was wainscoting bead board covered over with wall board. At the same time I had new electrical wiring and recessed lighting added to the kitchen ceiling and finally brought the wiring up to code.

I tore the lath and plaster from my bedroom walls and had them replaced by a local builder, the same builder who was getting rich from my house. During the time I was tearing my bedroom walls apart I was taking a drawing class, so for a project I sketched a wall without the lath and plaster, but before the insulation and sheet rock were in place. There were some pieces of lath on the left side, so I included them in the picture. Of course the picture isn't to scale. The wall here is about 7 feet, 6 inches tall and about 9 or 10 feet wide. It goes from the wall on the left to a window on the right.

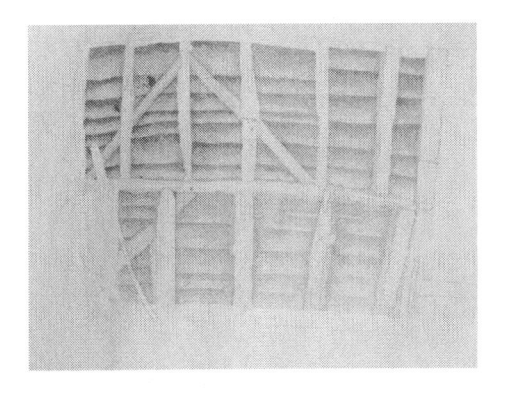

As time went by I was able to replace all of the plaster walls with sheet rock and of course I added insulation and upgraded the electrical service as I went.

Since I seem to have a habit of doing before thinking, one summer when it was really hot, I decided that I must have an air conditioner. I went to Montgomery Wards to buy the biggest one they had.

When I got it home, I realized that it would only fit in the front bay window, and it was so heavy I couldn't get it out of my car by myself. Tony removed it from my car and installed it into the window. This was kind of dangerous because the window was so close to the road.

Sometime in 1992 I realized that my well had been drilled on a piece of property along the north side of my house that the town actually owned. I approached the town and asked if I could buy the small piece, since it wasn't big enough for anyone to do anything with. It was given to the town by a man who had always lived in Pleasant Valley, and it was supposed to be kept un-developed so that the fire company could get water from the creek, or people could have a way to walk to the creek for tours given by the library. The fire company had not been using this access to get water, but from off the bridge instead. Although I never knew of the library giving any tours, I didn't object to this condition. I promised that I would let the property remain undeveloped and allow any access that was needed if they would sell it to me. I offered the town $100.

    I made the mistake of telling them that my well was on the property, and that's why I needed it. There was a monument to the local war veterans, which the local American Legion maintained between that piece of property and the state road. When the members of the American Legion learned that I was trying to buy this piece of property they objected because they were concerned that I wouldn't let them expand the monument area if they needed to. No matter how much I tried to explain to them that wouldn't be the case they held their ground. There would have to be a referendum on the election ballot before I could legally purchase the property. I felt I had to withdraw my offer. I was sure no one would vote for me over the American Legion.

      The state road that ran to the north of my property had a bridge over the Wappinger Creek which ran along the west edge of my property. The state decided they needed to replace the existing bridge and widen the road. As the plans for the bridge rebuilding progressed, the town decided that they would build a town park on the west side of the Wappinger Creek where a mill had stood, and move the war memorial to that spot as a focal point for the park. The mill where fabric was dyed had been one of the main employers in Pleasant Valley over the years. It had been abandoned and had burned a few years before. This relieved the American Legion members so they stopped their objection to my purchase of the property where my well was. I went back to the town to purchase the property. This time I was told that I would have to pay more money. I offered $300 in April 1997, but since there was an improvement on the property, namely my well, they said no, so I offered $1000. The town finally accepted $1300 which they said was the assessed value on the new tax rolls. I had to agree since I needed to own my well. February 1998 I purchased the property from the town for $1300. Later that year the state paid me $900 for the use of that piece of property so they could take down the old bridge and build a new one. Over the next two years the state tore down the old bridge, widened the road and erected a new bridge. Before they left they graded my back yard, planted a few pine trees, and black topped my driveway and another one on the west side of my house.

      Tony and his friends used the rocks that were left behind from the building of the bridge to create beautiful gardens in our new back yard by carrying rocks and making flower beds with paths between.

These are the gardens near the creek.

This is one of his small gardens.

I purchased several filter systems to try to get the sulfur out of my water, but never completely succeeded. Although we all bathed in the water, we drank bottled water and always went to a laundromat with our laundry. When the mint started the state quarters, I started collecting them for my grandkids. I have kept them in special folders to protect and organize them, the fumes from the sulfur water still got to them even in their protective folders and all but the few I have collected since I have been in Missouri are tarnished from the fumes of the sulfur water.

    As with any old house more and more repairs were needed. I retired in 2002, had less money and was making more trips to Missouri to see Karen and the kids. Even with financial help from Tony the bills were more than I was able to afford. Tony had started back to college and didn't have time for the yard care that was needed. I didn't have the physical strength to keep it all up. Sometime around 2004 I decided that I needed to sell my house and move to Missouri. Although I had planned to remain in this house until I died then give it to Tony, it had become an albatross around my neck.

    Over the years as the value of the house increased I refinanced several times. By the end the mortgage was $100,000 plus a home equity line of credit. I continued to live in that house, along with my son, until 2006 when I sold it to a friend for $144,000.00, which was only about $2000 less than I owed on it. I moved to Columbia, Missouri, so that I could be closer to Karen and my grandchildren. Tony is still in Pleasant Valley working and attending college. My friend is very happy, and due to modern chemistry she has succeeded in removing the sulfur from the water.

    I am also very happy; I am near my grand kids. I rent a very nice two bedroom duplex; all on one floor. I have a garage, a laundry room with washer and dryer, city water and sewer. I don't know which I appreciate most.

Living In Archie

It was 1972, and my husband Frank was out of work. Since his brother could get him a job at Owens Corning Fiberglass in Kansas City, Kansas, we sold our house in Pleasant Valley, my hometown and packed our belongings. We flew to Kansas City with our children: Karen who was seven at the time, and Tony who was about four and a half. Frank's brother met us at the airport and we went to Archie, Missouri, which would be our new home. At the time I looked at it as an adventure and it was. Frank's brother Harvey and his sister-in-law Zina were wonderful and welcoming to us. When we first arrived, we stayed with them until we found a house to rent. We got settled and looked for a house to buy.

Archie was a small town, covering about one square mile on the edge of the Kansas border, much smaller and different from anyplace I had ever seen. The sign at the edge of town read "Archie" on the first line, and "pop. 525" on the next line. The land all around was very flat, much different than where I had grown up in the Hudson Valley in New York State where there are hills and mountains. Main Street in Archie was wide, with cars parked at an angle to the curb. The curb was a foot high, maybe more. When there weren't many cars parked, the street looked extra wide. The railroad tracks ran parallel to Main Street, about half a block to the east. At one end of Main Street was a car wash with corrugated tin held by posts on each side and a narrow building with a door in the middle between the two lanes where cars parked while being washed. There were the usual hoses suspended high overhead so that you could wash all sides of the car without moving it. It was totally self-service and looking in need of repair. There was a wheat field next to it. During weekends and after school the local teens would hang-out at the car wash and drive up and down Main Street. Next to the car wash was the little house where Rosie lived. Sometimes Rosie used to baby sit our children. Along the main street were a Post Office, a barber shop, Day's Sundry's, a Laundromat, a library, a general store on the corner, and a small park for the kids to play at with some swings. Behind the library along the railroad tracks was the grain elevator, where the farmers brought their grain so it could be loaded onto the train. The town hall and police station were on the opposite end of Main Street from the car wash. There were also a few buildings containing businesses, that were closed. Most of the stores had awnings built onto the front. There were four streets running east and west, all named for trees: Elm, Walnut, Chestnut, and Pine. According to what I remember, the streets running parallel to Main Street were numbered streets like First and Second, but when I looked on the internet at maps.google.com those streets had the names of states on the west side of Main Street, and presidents on the east side of Main Street. There were four churches in Archie - the same number as in the town I came from with a population of about 9,000. There weren't any bars or liquor stores in the town. It was a "dry" town. That was really a strange concept for me to understand. A town without any alcohol sold anywhere. What were they thinking?

    As promised Frank got a job with Harvey, about 50 miles north on Interstate 71. They worked rotating shifts, but were on the same alternating schedule, between nights, days, and evenings with two or three days off between shifts, so they could ride together most of the time.

    The first house we rented was big and old, it was about a block from the school. There was a kitchen and living room and two large bedrooms. It would have been a very nice house if it didn't have a hole in the living room floor. There was a porch the length of the house on the east side, and a smaller one on the south side or front of the house.

We had a mouse in the kitchen. He seemed very cute in the beginning, with big ears but the more I thought about him, walking around on my silverware and dishes and leaving little "droppings" around the more I didn't think he was cute anymore but needed to be killed! He just wouldn't accept the cheese we left in the trap for him. He just came and went as he pleased through the hole in the living room floor. The only way to resolve the problem was for us to move out and leave him behind.

We bought a house on Chestnut Street, which was the same street, but across town from where Harvey and Zina lived. We lived on East Chestnut, they lived on West Chestnut.

Karen, Angie, Kelly, Tony ready for school.

After we moved we remained friends with our neighbors Pat and Charles Anderson, who had lived across the street. They had three kids: Spike who was about Tony's age, Kelly who was Karen's age, and Angie who was a little older.

The house did need work. The floors sagged, but didn't have holes like the previous one. It was located on a corner lot at the south east edge of the city, and had a big kitchen with no mice. There was a narrow stairway that led up to the rooms that became Karen and Tony's bedrooms. Frank brought home insulation for the unfinished walls upstairs but never got any farther than putting up the insulation. The walls remained studs with insulation between.

Sometimes Frank and Charles would go "noodleing" in the Grand River, which looked like a muddy stream to me. Since I was used to the Hudson River, I didn't know rivers could be so small. "Noodleing" is when you get into the water and reach up under the the banks of the river or in holes along the sides and grab fish with your hands. They had favorite places to go, and sometimes Pat would even go along and get into the water to block the fish from swimming away. It was certainly too scary for me. There were times that they would catch catfish as long as Tony was tall. Pat would clean them and cut them up for fried catfish. She would dip the fish in corn meal and fry it in lard. It might not have been good for our arteries, but it sure tasted good. Put fish together with some potato salad, some green beans cooked up with ham or bacon and several cans of beer, boy what a picnic that made!

One time while we were living in the house on the corner, Pat saw in the paper that some farmer was selling old laying hens for $1 each. She encouraged me to come along, and we would buy a couple to cook up for stew. We drove out to the farm and bought a few hens. They were alive so we had to kill them when we got them home. I wasn't sure how to go about that since the only way I was familiar with killing chickens was when I was a kid and my father used to cut their heads off with an ax on an old stump. He then let them run around like chickens with their heads cut off until they fell over. My mother's job had been to dip the chickens into boiling water, pluck the feathers and clean them. As we got ready in

An Eclectic Life

my back yard, Pat, with her cut off jeans and bare feet, took charge since she had more experience in actually doing the job. She took on the killing job by stepping on the chicken's head with her bare foot while she held the hen by it's legs, then giving a quick strong pull! Off came the head, and then she let the chicken run around just like my father used to. We were each going to pluck and clean our own chickens. The cleaning part wasn't hard for me, but I couldn't stand the heat so Pat plucked mine and hers.

Frank's mother, father and brother, John wanted to move out of Kansas City, so we bought the house next door on East Chestnut and moved into that so they could move into our house on the corner.

That house was in the best shape of all the houses we lived in during our time in Archie. We stayed there for the rest of our time in Archie. There was a very big back yard. Pat and Charles helped me by tilling up some garden space. I planted a pretty big garden with green beans, potatoes, onions, peas, and tomatoes, which produced good crops. I also planted Brussels sprouts and cauliflower, neither of which did very well, also some of the smallest broccoli you could imagine. I remember washing it really well, I thought, only to have what seemed like hundreds of little green worms come to the surface as I cooked it.

When I was getting ready to leave Pleasant Valley, one of my friends had asked about border collies. I told her that I would find one and bring it back for her. The first summer that we lived in Archie, I searched around and found a border collie to bring home to my friend. That year Karen, Tony & I took the train from Kansas City to New York while the puppy stayed in an animal crate in another part of the train. From New York to Poughkeepsie, the puppy was in a box with holes. I don't remember much about the trip. I think I blocked it out because it wasn't fun, except that we did get to Penn Station in New York City and Uncle George met us at the train and helped us get to Grand Central Terminal for the train to Poughkeepsie. My friend was very happy with the dog, until it started chewing things, and chasing other things. It ate one of her chickens, and she ended up having to give it away. The dog wasn't at all suited to living with chickens. It seems that there are places around the country known as "puppy farms" or "puppy mills" where some breeds or dogs are bred indiscriminately so their bad traits are what show up. It turns out that's where I found that one.

    Before I moved to Archie I didn't have a drivers license, I really didn't have any interest in driving. I liked to drink, and decided that I and everyone else would be better off if I didn't drive. After I lived in Archie for a while, I realized that I really needed to be able to get out of town when I wanted to instead of being dependant on other people. I decided that I would get a license. At the time we had a white Ford pick-up truck with blue trim that we purchased when we arrived in Archie. It was pretty large, and had a cap on the back so I had to learn to back up using the big side mirrors. The first time that I started out to go to Harrisonville to take my test, I stopped at the post office on the way to mail a letter. Instead of getting out of the car, it seemed a good idea to me to pull up to the outside mail box. Well, it wasn't such a good idea as it turned out since I misjudged and knocked the side mirror off the truck, thus postponing my driver's test until the mirror was fixed. I did successfully pass my driver's test and get my license. Frank got me a big light green Ford Country Squire station wagon with simulated wood grain along the sides.

    One time as I was preparing for a trip back to Pleasant Valley I got the idea to get some Coors beer for my friends back home. Coors wasn't available east of Kansas, so I went over

An Eclectic Life

the Kansas border to a bar and bought several cases of it. Before I got them all packed into the car I got together with our friends Pat and Charles to drink some of my very special Coors beer. As soon as they looked at the top of the cans they told me I had made a mistake! Clearly stamped on the top of each can in red ink was the fact that it was 3.2% alcohol! The normal alcohol content of beer is 5%. I found out, a little late. In Kansas if you want your beer to be normal 5%, you need to buy it at a state ABC store not a bar.

I was bored with my life in Archie, so I looked for things to fill it during the day while the kids were in school.

In April 1975 I ran for Mayor of Archie, but I failed to get elected. This is the ad from the local paper:

Meet Pat Holt

Pat is a mayoral candidate in next week's city election. A three-year resident of Archie, Pat, her husband, Frank, their children, Karen and Tony, came here from Pleasant Valley, New York, which is Pat's home town. Pat likes our home town and has taken an active interest in community affairs since locating here.

Pat is 35, a U.S. Marine from 1959 to 1962. She is presently active as Cass County PTA Historian, Cass County Chairman of Public Education of the American Cancer Society, 3rd year Chairman for Archie's Cancer Drive, a Registered Emergency Medical Technician regularly working with Archie's Ambulance Volunteers and a member of St. Peter's Episcopal Church in Harrisonville. Having just completed Nursing Assistant's Training, Pat is employed at the Countryside Nursing Home in Butler.

Pat is honest, energitic, inquisitive, concerned, committed to her beliefs. Having no conflicts of interest or business affiliation, Pat is available and responsive to the needs of people and the community.

Archie's need for more direction of leadership is evidenced by the views expressed to Pat by her citizens. Among those:
- More cooperation and openness between the council and citizenry.
- Efforts to meet requirements and obtain use of Federal Grants to improve our city. We pay taxes toward these funds—we should benefit.
- Organization, training and adequate equipment to sustain fire protection.
- Enforcement of the Dog Ordinance.
- Continuous love and care to the small city park—it's there, but unfit and unhealthy for children to play.
- Roadside weeds mowed regularly.
- Consistent and common sense zoning regulations.
- Long range plans for recreation facility including a swimming pool and park.
- A beautification and clean-up program.
- Decisions based on facts—not on fears and prejudice.
- A change of leadership.

Archie needs a change of leadership. Pat is offering her time and energy and will serve with intergrity and openness.

VOTE FOR PAT ON TUESDAY, APRIL 1, 1975.
(Ad paid for by friends of Pat Holt for Mayor.)

I worked for a short while at a storm window and door factory on an assembly line, then at the Countryside Nursing Home in Butler, MO. While I had been living in Archie I had also been volunteering as an EMT with the volunteer ambulance. The ambulance that they used had been a hearse and was modified. I thought about becoming a nurse so I could help people. I knew since I was a Marine Corps veteran I could get financial help to go to school. I thought they would only pay if I passed whatever courses I took, so I was afraid to attempt to get the benefits. I decided to check into the real story and found out that I could get an allowance to cover my family of four, while I attended school. It didn't matter what my grades were as long as I was attending an accredited program. The funds would run out March 1976. Too bad I didn't check sooner.

I signed up for LPN classes at the Vocational Technical School in Nevada, Missouri, and started classes in the summer of 1975. The school was about 50 miles south of Archie down Highway 71. I met a couple of women in my class that were from Adrian, which was the next town south of Archie. I picked them up on the way, and we took turns driving. At the time I had a big green Ford Country Squire station wagon, so there was plenty of room. All of our trips were uneventful, except two times. Once when I had a blow-out while going 70 miles per hour down the highway. When I heard bang, I made the mistake of stomping on the breaks. When I did that, the car went out of control and we were swerving all over the road. Lucky for all of us, I took my foot off the brake and coasted to a stop at the edge of the road without hitting anything. The other time was when I hadn't latched my hood well after I had checked something in the motor. As I picked up speed, there was a loud noise and my visibility was gone! The hood flew up and covered the whole area of the windshield so that I couldn't see anything. I pulled over to the side of the road. Together we pulled the hood as closed as we could, tied it to hold it down, and continued on the highway to school.

    We had classes in physiology, anatomy, and patient care. We also had classes on death and dying. For the death and dying class we used <u>On Death and Dying</u> by Elisabeth Kubler-Ross. We also spent time in a 50 bed hospital practicing. Because the hospital was small, we got to have a lot of hands on training.

    It was normal practice to shave a woman's pubic hair before she gave birth. I remember doing that on one occasion. It was the young lady's first baby, and I told her it was my first time of ever shaving a person. I don't suppose that made her very comfortable. We got to stay with the patient into the delivery room, and witness the miracle of birth. That might have been the best moment during my whole learning experience. There were some older people in the hospital that we practiced on. One time when we were learning about catheterizations, there was a lady who was from a nursing home and unconscious for some reason that I'm not sure of now. It was my turn to do a catheterization, so I put on gloves, covered the area with the sterile cloth that came in the kit that we used. Even though we had seen pictures and demonstrations of the proper technique, I proceeded to insert the catheter into the wrong spot! As soon as I realized what I had done, I quickly removed it and inserted it correctly into the urethra. My supervisor was quite shocked, and told me I was supposed to leave that tube inserted, and insert another one into the urethra, and then remove the one I had placed into her vagina. What I did could have caused an infection, but luckily for all of us it didn't, and since the patient was unconscious she never knew what happened.

    One day while I was getting ready for school, I had an itch just below my right breast, and discovered a pea-sized lump. I was nervous enough to have it checked, but didn't think it was cancer because I had seen a breast biopsy that turned out to be cancer. The surgeon during that operation made the comment that when the tumor is separate from the tissue it is most likely benign. When the tissue has enlarged it is more likely malignant. My lump was like someone had placed a little hard pea under my skin. I reported it to the doctor, who scheduled the surgery. The lump was removed, and I was correct it was benign.

I was going to school all week, and having to study when I got home, Frank worked rotating shifts between nights, evenings, and days with two or three days off between shift changes. It was a very erratic schedule. His family lived in Kansas City. He had one niece who was fifteen and two younger ones. Their parents wanted to get them out of the city into the safer environment of a small town, so it was decided that they should come live with us and to go to school in Archie. Beverly could help with the kids when Frank and I were at work. When Beverly and her sister Sherry moved in, we moved Tony into a small room, and the girls shared the bigger bedroom with Karen. Sometimes Beverly would even fix dinner. The only meal I actually remember her fixing though was Tuna Helper - macaroni and cheese with tuna added. Things seemed to be working pretty well until I began to notice Frank and Beverly were spending more and more time together. One day Karen told me she saw them kissing. I confronted him and told him that he must move Beverly out, and he should leave too. He moved to Kansas City and stayed with his sister and brother-in-law(Beverly's parents.)

I filed for divorce and since he didn't respond in 30 days, papers were served on him at his job because I didn't know exactly where he was living. Thirty days after he signed the divorce papers I went with my lawyer to the county court building in Harrisonville, Missouri, and verified in court that it was his signature, and we were given a divorce for irreconcilable differences. I got the house, my car, and most of our belongings. We split the bills that we owed. He was supposed to pay child support but I am not sure how much he actually paid.

After we were divorced he got involved with a divorced woman who lived in Archie. He married her, and moved in with her. During that time Karen and Tony used to see him, and spend time with him.

I continued my education during and after my divorce. When I needed someone to watch my kids they either stayed with Rosie, who lived near the car wash or Pat, who lived near the school.

When I graduated from LPN school, I sold the house. With Frank's help I loaded everything I owned into a U-Haul, packed up the kids, and moved back to Pleasant Valley. I found out that when you pack a U-Haul the load should be even, not too much to the front, and do not have re-tread tires on your car. The combination may cause the tread to start peeling away from the tires due to the heat generated. That is what happened to me. Fortunately for me a neighbor had given me a pair of extra tires, so somewhere during the middle of the trip I had to go to a garage and get the back tires of my car changed.

Soon after the kids and I left, Frank left the woman he had married in Archie and moved back in with his niece. They moved to Denver, Colorado. While he was there he had a very good job and during that time he was sending me $100 each month. About a year later he disappeared for several years.

When we returned to Pleasant Valley, we stayed with my aunt Toddy until I found a place for us to live. I tried to get a job as an LPN, but there weren't any available in the local hospitals. I was able to find a job at an adult care facility near where we were living. It was where the unemployment office sent me since there weren't openings for LPN jobs. I worked there for a few months helping in the kitchen and cleaning the living areas. The pay was minimum wage and the job was boring.

As soon as the nursing license test was scheduled to be given in Albany, New York, I went and took the test. I passed it and was officially a Licensed Practical Nurse. I continued to look for work in my field. That is when I applied at Harlem Valley Psychiatric Center and was hired there.

I am glad for my time in Archie. I wish things had been different, but as I look back, there were more positive experiences than negative ones.

Me with my nurses cap.

During the summer of 2008 I drove back to Archie to see how the town looked and to see if anyone I knew was still there. The only person that I found that I knew was my former sister-in-law Zina. As I stopped in the driveway of what used to be the house where she and Harvey lived, I felt very nervous. I wasn't sure if she was still there or if she was, how she would greet me. She was still living in the same house that she lived in 32 years ago when I left Archie. She was 83 years old and widowed since Harvey died in 1993. She had a riding lawnmower and a regular one so that she could keep the very large lawn mowed. Sometimes her son came and helped her. He lived out in the country and worked on a farm, plus he had a job as a mechanic. Her daughters have all grown and have children of their own, even her granddaughter has two children. It was nice to sit and visit with her, and catch up on my in-laws. She invited me back sometime when we could go out to eat, and I could spend the night if I wanted to.

  The Main Street has several abandoned stores. The grocery store had a restaurant built into it. The library was well kept and had a mural painted on the side. The building next to it was a video rental store which was painted white, and had a mural painted on the side toward the library. The park with picnic tables between the two buildings looked like a very pleasant place to sit. There was a large, new hardware store, and some new storage buildings. The old car wash where the local kids used to hang out looked abandoned. The school had grown very large, and across from it in what used to be our back yard there were two large tablets containing the Ten Commandments. By the look of the new homes people have moved out of Kansas City and commute from Archie. The local restaurant had changed owners. There still weren't any taverns in the town that I could see, but the gas station did sell beer.

These are a few of my political buttons from past years.

Political Me

With tears in my eyes and hope in my heart I listened to Jennifer Hudson sing the national anthem, and thought, what a song! When it is sung by someone with such a strong voice, I am always inspired. The Democratic National Convention started and officially nominated a black man, Barack Obama, to run for President of the United States.

How far we have come since my days in the Marine Corps, I remember waiting out side the bus terminal with the black girls in my platoon, after graduating from Marine Corps boot camp, because they couldn't wait inside in North Carolina, of seeing the "colored only" and "white only" drinking fountains first hand and watching the racial violence of the 1960's on the television. It fills my heart with such joy and gratitude for the people of this country that we have come this far.

When I was in high school girls weren't even allowed to play basketball on the whole court, due to the worry that we were so delicate we might get "the vapors," now to see a woman be respected by so many as Hillary Clinton made 18 million cracks in the glass ceiling. Her courage and tenacity in her run for the presidential nomination were inspirational.

I felt hope for this country like I haven't for several years.

When I grew up what I knew about politics was that uncle Fred was the town clerk. He was a Democrat. Members of the town board came to his house sometimes and met in his dining room, local politicians gave Hershey bars to the kids and maybe the women too, and White Owl cigars to men at election time. I knew political nepotism existed; it was a fact of life, so I didn't even think of it as wrong. It was who you knew, not what you knew. The farmers were Republicans, so if it was sunny on Election Day they would stay home and work, that meant it was a good day for the Democrats. It must have been sunny on a lot of election days, because my uncle Fred was re-elected as town clerk every time he ran; he finally retired after serving 32 years in office.

The Town Clerk Office was in his home, he had two very big safes in the dining room to keep all the records in. I think one of the points that made him electable, besides the sunny election days, was that he could always be found. He didn't have specific office hours, if you needed hunting or fishing licenses and he wasn't at home you could find him at the local bar and he would have his license book with him.

I guess you could say I grew up a Democrat, since that was what my family was and I didn't know any different.

By the time I got out of the Marine Corps I became a Republican. It was a combination of my military training and the influence of my boy friend, soon to be husband, that caused this shift. He thought Barry Goldwater was wonderful; I still have my "AuH2O button from 1964. My husband had lived in Arizona when he joined the Marine Corps; Barry Goldwater was his senator and had helped him keep from getting a dishonorable discharge from the Marine Corps for bigamy. Uncle George told me, when he found out that I had registered Republican, he was going to cut me out of his will.

I also have buttons for "Nixon's the One!", "Reagan '76", and Buckley with an American flag. Around 1980 I ran for a council seat in my hometown of Pleasant Valley, New York on the Republican ticket. I didn't get elected which, looking back, I'm glad of.

During the Vietnam War I was sure we were doing the right thing and anyone who opposed the war was not patriotic. I was infuriated when I saw the protesters and other long haired hippy types wearing military jackets. I didn't understand what they were thinking to disgrace the uniform that my relatives and I had worn so proudly. My nephew and cousin were in Vietnam fighting for what I considered an important cause. If my government thought it was right, it must be!

    By the time Bill Clinton ran for president in 1992, I was ready to vote Democrat. Actually, I just found a "Read My Lips No Bush In '92" button, so I guess that's when I changed. I'm not even sure what caused my change of heart, maybe wisdom came with age. Maybe I had a change of heart because I had quit drinking and was seeing the world through clearer eyes.

Pictured above are John Livingston and his friend Ollie. This is the house they worked on for "Diggie and Lloyd in Pearlington.

Rebuilding Pearlington

On August 29, 2005, as I watched the news, I saw the awful devastation in New Orleans from hurricane Katrina.

I understand the power of water, as it rampages through a town. I was a teenager in 1955 when a flood devastated my town, Pleasant Valley, New York. I watched in horror as water flowed through houses, into the back windows and doors, and out the front. The sight of live cows fighting against the current, and trees rushing by in the swiftly flowing flood water burned into my memory forever.

My first instinct upon hearing the news of Katrina was to go to the Red Cross to get a collection can to collect money to help. It didn't seem like much, but going down to New Orleans to help or organizing truck loads of goods to be shipped down didn't seem like anything I could do. So I got the collection can, and collected what I could.

Sometime later in the fall, my friend Darlene, active in "Habitat for Humanity," told me about an opportunity to go to the little town of Pearlington, Mississippi, where Habitat was organizing home rebuilding, and I started planning for my trip.

At first I thought I wouldn't have enough carpenter skills to be helpful. I knew, from working on a Habitat build in my area, however, that there would be skilled people willing to help. If nothing else I could paint.

At the end of January I loaded my car with my paint brushes, blankets and pillow. I added Darlene's carpenter tools, and sleeping bag. She was flying down, so I brought her things for her.

I went by way of Columbia, Missouri, to visit my daughter and grandkids. While there, I gathered some items I thought I would need, like her tent, propane stove, frying pan, camp coffee pot, and air mattress. I also purchased plenty of film for my camera, safety glasses, hammer, and nail belt for my work on the houses.

On February 10, 2006 I started the 850 mile trip from my daughter's house to Pearlington, Mississippi. Pearlington is a very small town; according to the 2000 census Pearlington had about seventeen hundred people, and eight hundred thirty housing units. It is about ten miles inside the Mississippi/Louisiana state border, very near the gulf and the Pearl River, which both overflowed during hurricane Katrina, and about a one hour drive from New Orleans.

I arrived in the nearby town of Slidell, Louisiana, which had been a city of about twenty-six thousand, but now looked like a ghost town with empty and boarded up buildings everywhere. I called Darlene; and we drove around this nearly abandoned city separately, we found each other by describing where we each were on our cell phones. We finally met at an Outback for supper before we ventured into Pearlington. The only places in Slidell serving food were the big name chains; the smaller places were still closed and boarded up because of the flood.

On either side of the road into the town of Pearlington stood large trees with Spanish moss hanging from the branches, their Spanish moss looked tattered. Some of these trees had broken branches, and sometimes items of clothing or trash lodged high up in them.

We drove into town in our little caravan of two, and found the Charles B. Murphy School where we would be staying for the week. As I looked around the large room that would be our bedroom, shared with 10 other women, I realized that it had once been the school library, and the only windows were two in the wall opposite from the door, and neither of them were the kind that could be opened. One window contained a kind of an electric heater I had never seen before.

There were at least 20 aluminum cots arranged against the cement block walls, and about eight more in the middle of the room. There was also a little 5 foot by 5 foot space with a curtain for the modest among us to change clothes in.

Darlene and I chose cots that were located in the corner, to the left when you entered the room, and since there was clearly an overabundance of mattresses, we also each took two mattresses for our cots.

The bathrooms were 2 port-a-potties across the parking lot. Outside the port-a-potties were a foot pump faucet and a sink for hand washing. Next to them was a structure made of plywood and 2 x 4's with a blue tarp roof that contained 2 washer and dryer sets, arranged back to back. There was a hand painted sign on it that read "Laundromat." Next in the line of amenities was a trailer, which contained separate showers for men and women. There were large square water containers that supplied the water for the showers. As I remember there wasn't any lighting provided, except what came in through the windows. Just past the shower trailer there were 2 more port-a-potties. I was thinking, *"This is going to present a problem for someone like me who always needs to pee in the middle of the night!"*

Soon, other volunteers who were part of Habitat for Humanity of Dutchess County, New York, arrived. I was glad to know some of them, and especially glad for a good friend of mine who had the same "peeing in the middle of the night" problem as I did. We made a pact to go together in the night!

It was quite cold there, so when we made our trip across the parking lot, we needed to wear our clothes, or at least shoes, and a jacket over our pajamas. It was good to have company as I ventured out across the parking lot the first few nights, as we got used to the trek in the night, we soon felt safe to go by ourselves. During the first night I discovered that the heater in the window didn't have a thermostat so it ran constantly once it was turned on, causing the room to become overheated and stuffy, but warm weather came abruptly in the middle of the week we didn't have to use the heater very much.

We were soon joined by a group of young women from the Walter Hoving House, which is a Christian community for women recovering from addictions, in Putnam County, New York.

They were a friendly group who brought snacks with them, both were very welcome, since there weren't any stores for us to buy junk food and it was pretty quiet in our big bedroom.

The Red Cross food tent provided meals for residents and volunteers until February 15, 2006. They cooked in a separate tent and brought the food into the dining tent in insulated containers. They had been serving food for 6 months since the hurricane. When they left there was a food trailer that was set up by a Christian group. This was manned by several middle aged men who were very nice but, not used to cooking for large groups. The first meal they provided was breakfast, and it consisted of coffee and oatmeal, or pancakes. I choose the oatmeal and coffee.

A group of men from a church in Colorado drove down in a small bus with a trailer full of equipment. They stayed in another part of the school. They did whatever was needed around the town like cutting up trees, or helping fix plumbing problems. Before the local residents could get a FEMA trailer, they needed to show that they had water and sewer hook-ups ready, and since there weren't any plumbers in business to be called, they needed volunteer help.

There was a store set up to provide free canned food and other supplies that had been donated by various church groups around the country. They called the store "Pearlmart," and it was located in what had been the school gym. There was a high water mark on the basketball backstop to show how high the flood waters had been. One of the ladies who worked there had come down with her husband from Miamisburg, Ohio. They came with their camper to see what help they could be. He was helping as a handyman around town, and she was working in the store.

Part of our group worked on the house that would be occupied by a lady called "Diggie" and her husband Lloyd. To show her gratitude and hospitality she used to make lunch and snacks for the volunteers who worked on her house. Lloyd was in a wheel chair, so they were very cramped in their little FEMA trailer. They never complained about the situation they were in; they were just grateful for the help from all over the country that had been offered to them.

I have never seen such destruction. Did you know that when ceiling fans get wet, they droop, like dying flowers? It still brings tears to my eyes to look at the pictures of "Diggie" and Lloyd's home, that I was sure had been neat and tidy, now with the ceiling fan drooping, and the family pictures on the wall, fading from being wet with the flood waters. There were some cleaning supplies and dish soap still on the kitchen counter. Perhaps she or her daughter had started to clean, but it was too overwhelming, and couldn't be done by dish soap alone.

Fan in Diggie and Lloyd's house.

    Soon after we left, this house was featured on CBS TV as a finished home, and Diggie and her husband were shown receiving the keys to their new home, provided by New Hope Construction and Habitat for Humanity. It made for good publicity, and encouraged people to give donations, but when I returned to visit two months later, they weren't quite into their house yet! There were several problems that were still being worked on

    Since there wasn't any running water in many of the houses around town, there were blue port-a-potties on several street corners. They served very useful not only for their intended use, but also as landmarks, since most of the street signs were gone. I knew the house I was working on was the next right turn after the port-a-potty near the house with big buses in the yard.

    The house I had worked on was actually part of two matching houses that would be connected and occupied by an extended family, including the husband's father. The family that would move into the house I was working on was living with relatives because they had school aged children. That way the children could attend school, and it would be more comfortable than living in the FEMA trailer, seeing the destruction all the time.

Most of the people in the town had gone to the NASA center nearby to "ride out the storm." One of the people who stayed was Eugene Keyes. He was in a wheelchair, because both of his legs had been amputated below the knees, due to diabetes. He was currently living in a FEMA trailer, with his brother. He told me the amazing story of his survival. He and his brother were staying in a house in town, an old time log cabin. He said that although it had been raining and storming, it seemed to clear a little, so he went out on the porch with his coffee to look around. All of a sudden he heard a loud roar, and looked up to see a twenty foot wall of water coming into town! He said he hurried back into the house, in his electric wheelchair. He got into the house, but the water was quickly up his chest, and his wheelchair shorted out.

He got hold of an antique rocking chair and floated up to grab onto a beam. He remained there, and prayed to God, until the water receded. Since he lost both his prosthetic legs during the flood he had to have his brother shove a book case under him to help get him down. He and his brother, who is also over 70 years old, were stranded in the house for 2 days. They had only the food they could find in the house to eat; that included a jar of peanut butter that came floating past.

Mr. Keyes said that while he was hanging onto the beam he only saw one snake in the house, and a big fish floated by. He also said that when he looked out the glass door, he saw an alligator about 12 feet long, and he prayed to God that the glass door wouldn't break; and it didn't!

House Mr. Keyes was in.

Another part of our group helped an Iraq war veteran who was home from Iraq due to shrapnel injuries. The house that they worked on belonged to his brother. His brother could not rebuild his own home because he needed to work to earn money for the repairs and to feed his family. The family had evacuated during the flood, and when they returned they found that their home had been a refuge for three families during the flood. The entire house had to be "gutted" and sprayed with mold retardant before it could be rebuilt and made livable. The debris from the house had to be transported down the road and placed along the highway where it was added long piles of trash to be removed.

The local bar, "Turtle Landing," was destroyed during the flood, but had re-opened in a large tent in the yard of the original bar. The original building was still standing, but the front of the upstairs living quarters had been ripped off. It was quite a sight. The beams were showing, the windows were still nailed in place, and parts of the tar paper from under the siding still showed. As you approached the temporary bar, there were two blue port-a-potties to the right of the entrance, and a large trash container near the door of the tent. The tent looked like the kind that is used for a garage with a large opening in the front. The floor was made of plywood nailed to 2 x 4's and covered with green indoor/outdoor carpeting. Inside there were two tables with a very large crock-pot of beef stew, some rice, bread, plates, and plastic ware. The supper was free or for a donation and provided every Wednesday night. Alongside of the food tables there were three or four computer slot machines, and a Santa with a tie dyed shirt and Mardi Gras beads. A few local customers were at the bar.

I returned February, 2007, with Dutchess County Habitat for Humanity and found there was a lot of work still to be done throughout the town. The "Pearlmart" was still in business, and the lady that I had met on my previous trip who was from Miamisburg, Ohio was still working there. Diggie and Lloyd were having an addition put on their home so that she would have more room, and she was still quick to offer food or drink to everyone.

In 2007 instead of staying at the school in Pearlington, we stayed at a place called Camp Coastal. For $15 per night they provided bunk houses, breakfast, and dinner at a dining tent, and bag lunches to take with us to work. I joined a small group of Habitat for Humanity workers from New York. I only had to share the bunk house with one other woman. We had a bathroom and shower inside the bunk house. It was quite cold, and our heat consisted of one mini square electric heater. When we tried to use two at a time it blew the circuit breaker. The last morning we were there it was so cold that the water coming from the faucet in the bathroom froze when it hit the sink.

We also found that the Pearlington Baptist Church was open and was providing home cooked lunches to local residents and volunteers. The food was offered free, but there was a box for donations if you could afford it. That became our favorite place to eat lunch.

Camp Coastal was organizing home building in the gulf coast area, through the Coastal Domicile Replacement Program

(CDR). More than 100 homes were to be completed during the summer of 2007 in Mississippi and 40 homes in Louisiana, through the CDR. The project has involved thousands of volunteers, hundreds of professional laborers and the collaboration of dozen's of helping organizations, among them to the People of Saudi Arabia who, believing in this effort, provided $3.9 million in funding to supply materials and labor to underwrite the cost of the project. The houses they are building are larger and more permanent than the ones we were working on previously with Habitat and New Home Construction.

We worked on a very nice three bedroom home that was completely wheelchair accessible, with a large front porch, and a back deck. It was to be the new home for a family with an 8 year old girl who had been born with spina bifida, which caused her to have to use a wheelchair. Once again there was a lot of painting to be done, since when we arrived, nothing had yet been painted. The house still needed the electricity and plumbing connected. While we were there our crew completed most of what was needed, and the house was almost ready for the family to move in.

When I think back to my time there, I think some of the things that impressed me most were the spirit of the local people, and the outpouring of help from the various religious groups, and very little government help. This was an eye opening experience, I am glad I could help.

The following are two of the many scenes of destruction that I captured with my camera.

A normal scene of trash along the roads.

A trailer, car and a boat all in a field.

A house that had a statue of Mary on a brick pedestal in their yard, the house was destroyed but Mary remained standing.

The house rebuilt, with the statue still on the pedestal, now with a plaque "I survived Hurricane Katrina even though the water was over my head."

My Tomatoes

During the summer of 2005, when I sold photographs at the farmers markets in Poughkeepsie and Pleasant Valley, at times I got hungry, and a farm that sold tomatoes there, sold the biggest and best tomatoes I have ever eaten.

At the Pleasant Valley market. I would bring my own bread along with some mayonnaise, salt and pepper. At the Poughkeepsie market, I would buy crusty French bread, mozzarella cheese from other venders, and borrow a little olive oil from the importer. Sometimes, instead of olive oil, I would buy some homemade pesto. Then I would buy a large Italian heart heirloom tomato from Wilklow Orchard, a fruit and vegetable farm in Highland, New York. Italian Heart tomatoes made slices as large as a slice of bread, and had very few seeds and little of that watery tomato juice, just big hearty tomato slices. This made for a very yummy lunch, and it was something that I looked forward to at each market.

When I made the decision to sell my home in Pleasant Valley and move to Missouri, I thought I was very clever, because I saved some Italian heart tomato seeds to take with me. This way I would be able to grow my own Italian heart tomatoes, since I didn't know if I would be able to find them there.

During my first visit back to New York State, since it was spring it occurred to me that instead of searching for the seeds I'd brought with me I could buy plants already started at Wilklow Orchard. I looked up the orchard in the phone book and called to ask if they would sell me two plants. When Sharon said yes, I decided to go the next day to get my very special tomato plants. When I arrived Sharon wasn't at home, but she had left the plants for me as promised. I paid one dollar each, and drove back the curvy mountain road to Pleasant Valley. I went directly to my cousin Babs' house to show her my prize tomatoes. She agreed they'd need larger containers for their trip to Missouri, she had just the thing in her well stocked garden area. Babs has many beautiful flowers and a green thumb. Just at the edge of the woods by her house she has a compost pile, so she re-potted my young plants into larger pots with lots of good Pleasant Valley compost. I knew they should be happy and prosper.

During this part of my trip I was staying with Don and Judy Rielle who have a very nice home in Hyde Park, New York and very healthy tomato plants of their own in containers on their deck. Since my tomato plants were so special and were about to embark on a long journey half way across the USA, Judy thought it was only fitting that they should be named. It seemed like a very good idea to me, and we decided since Thelma and Louise were two famous women who traveled around the USA, that should be the basis for their names. Yet these were Italian heart tomatoes so the names became Theresa and Louisa.

As I looked at them sitting on the deck alongside Judy and Don's large healthy plants, I like many mothers began to compare my "Girls" with the plants near them, and my girls didn't look as healthy, the leaves were a little smaller, and not as dark green. My father would have called them "spindly."

I decided that since there was a Cornell University Cooperative Extension office nearby I would bring my precious girls there for a check up. Theresa was kept overnight to be studied by a Master Gardener. The next day when I picked her up and paid the six dollars, I got the diagnosis: "Too much salts/minerals in soil caused tip burn, can add some nitrogen when you get home. Leaves look yellow from lack of chlorophyll, too much watering. Need more sunlight, back off watering." The idea of too much water and not enough sun sounded good, but it did seem out of my control since they had been sitting outside, and would continue to be outside. Luckily for them the rain stopped and the sun came out. I carefully tended them and when it was time for me to leave for Missouri I settled them carefully in specially prepared boxes on the floor in the back seat of my Toyota Camry. There they would be most protected from the direct air conditioner breeze. I was concerned about stopping to eat along my journey west. I imagined that I wouldn't be able to stop for very long if it was hot since the temperature in the car would be bad for the girls. I decided that I would eat only things that I could bring back to the car and eat while driving or sit with the air conditioner on. Of course I couldn't allow it to get too cold inside the car either. My, this was taking a lot of planning.

    The weather cooperated, and I was able to get the girls to Columbia without incident. I carefully dug a large hole in my back yard. I removed the dirt because native soil here is full of clay, and didn't seem like a very good bed for my precious Theresa and Louisa. I searched the local stores for the correct soil. I found two bags of garden soil, there were pictures of tomatoes on the bag, so I figured this would be the kind of dirt that I needed. I brought the bags of dirt home, dumped one bag into the hole where the tomato plants would go, then carefully placed the plants about two feet apart, I filled in with the remaining bag of dirt. It looked from the list of ingredients on the bag that there should be enough nitrogen and other minerals to produce healthy plants with many yummy tomatoes.

    After a few weeks the plants seemed to be growing ok, but the blossoms were disappearing. I went to a local greenhouse and the very nice girl at the counter sold me a bottle of time release nitrogen balls, because extra nitrogen would be good for the plants, and a bottle of fungicide to spray on the plants in case there was a fungus present, and some very nice already grown ripe tomatoes. After I applied the little nitrogen balls and the fungicide the plants grew large and strong, and produced lots of blossoms, which continued to disappear. I returned to the same greenhouse, this time a man waited on me, and after I explained my problem he attempted to sell me deer repellent, because he said maybe deer were eating my tomato blossoms. I didn't agree with his conclusion so I didn't buy the $20 product he suggested. I was sure that deer wouldn't just nibble off the blossoms no matter how tasty they were. I did buy more very nice already grown ripe tomatoes.

By the middle of August I was at my wits end. I was now seeing blossoms, but they were shriveling and falling off. I turned to the internet, and decided from what I read there my precious girls had "blossom-drop". This meant that the blossoms just don't open correctly, and they don't get pollinated, so they fell off. Back to the store, and I purchased a spray on blossom set, and in case that wasn't enough I tried to pollinate them myself with a little paint brush, all to no avail.

One morning as I looked at them huddled together because of the wind, or maybe to protect themselves from me and my chemicals, I thought sadly of all the blossoms had come and gone. I wondered if they would ever bare fruit.

On August 24 as I was saying good morning to them, I noticed small bugs that looked like miniature walking sticks and saw parts of the plants hanging lifelessly. I decided that those bugs were somehow eating where the blossom was connected to the plants and causing the blossoms to fall off before they could set fruit. I got a spray bottle of nicotine juice from my daughter and started spraying to kill the bugs. It didn't help with the blossoms dropping off, but at least it was a free solution to my bug problem, since the bugs were gone.

In September I went to a tomato festival at the University of Missouri Extension farm office. I took some pieces from my plants to show the gardeners and was told I had given my tomatoes too much nitrogen, causing the plants to use all their energy to grow leaves, leaving none for producing tomatoes. Since there was no way to remove the extra nitrogen from the soil, I was told to try again next year.

Finally by the end of September as the weather began to cool small tomatoes were growing to about the size of golf balls. I asked about my tomato problems at the local farmers market, and was told that because of the relentless heat this summer in Columbia these heirloom tomatoes would not produce. I needed tomatoes that were specifically bred for this hot weather.

As the weather started to turn cold and frost was predicted, I covered them at night a few times, but then I decided to pick the tomatoes Theresa and Louisa had produced and bring them inside to ripen. I ended up with about a dozen green tomatoes, ranging in size from baseballs to golf balls. I put them in a quiet corner of my laundry room and waited and watched for the first blush of red. Finally, the first one looked ripe, it was small but maybe it would taste good anyway. I cut into it, and I noticed immediately that there was something strange about it; it was solid and seedless, more greenish-orange in color than red like it should be. I tasted it and my fears were confirmed, it tasted awful, kind of tart and bland at the same time. Not at all like the yummy Italian heart tomatoes that I remembered from New York.

During winter as I looked out at the skeletons of what were my precious Theresa and Louisa I saw little birds among the dried leaves pecking around in the soil. I like to believe that they are gaining nourishment from the blossoms that fell there all summer, or maybe those little nitrogen balls that were still visible on the ground.

    Not to be discouraged by my first experience growing tomatoes in Missouri, when spring came again I purchased native variety of tomatoes. They produced smaller but flavorful tomatoes.

The Dentist Visit

Oh no! There is something wrong in my mouth, or is it something in my chicken sandwich? It's the crown that used to be cemented to the far back bottom molar on the left. Is it loose in my mouth? No, maybe it is just a piece of chicken, or bread crust. I'll just carefully remove this food from my mouth, or maybe it's my imagination.

It's the crown! How could this happen? I just had my teeth checked and cleaned back in Pleasant Valley, New York, so that I wouldn't have to find a dentist here where I've moved in Missouri.

It's 5:05 on Friday night. Should I get in my car and drive back to Pleasant Valley? If I leave now, I can get there by Monday morning to see my dentist. But, my grandkids need me. I have to watch Brian Saturday and Sunday night, I have to pick up Robert Sunday from his father's. Brian has a birthday party Sunday afternoon; I have to take him to that. I have to pick April up for school on Monday morning at 7 AM.

I'll call my daughter. She'll know a dentist here I can call, but I hate to go to a new dentist.

She gave me the name of her dentist, and warned me that dentists are open fewer hours than banks. I found out how right she was when I got the message: "Our Office is closed now. Our regular hours are Monday to Thursday 10 AM to 4 PM, please call back." I left a message, and looked in the phone book for the dentist who advertises on the radio. His commercial makes him sound very kind and painless. "Dr. Colimalocker" I think that is what the kid in the commercial says. It's also called Sterling Dental Care. After some research I found the number. His name is Dr. Colin Malaker, and his office is very near my house. Of course he was also closed, so I left another message.

I ate very carefully over the weekend, and saved my old crown in a sandwich baggie.

Monday morning at 9:00 I called back the first dentist and made an appointment, the first I could make with him which was Wednesday afternoon, and then it seemed only after the receptionist was sure I had dental insurance. I decided that I would give that kind, painless- sounding Dr Colin Malaker a chance in case I could get an appointment with him sooner. I called, and was given an appointment at 10:00 AM that very day.

While I waited for my appointment time, I remembered my first experience with a dentist.

When I was young, I had chipped a front tooth while swimming and the dentist said I had to wait until I was a teenager to get it fixed, so when I was about 16 or 17 my father took me to the dentist.

The metal parts of the headrest pushed into my head while the dentist leaned over me as I sat in the dental chair. The room seemed crowded with equipment. There was a tiny sink near my left arm. In front of me there was a little tray with some scary looking picks. Big arms sprouted from a post with belts and scary drills on the ends. Silently the dentist checked my mouth and made the decision I needed a root canal and a permanent crown.

I'm not sure how many shots of novacaine I was given, but it still hurt a lot. Even the shots that I got in the roof of my mouth hurt every time. Since drills weren't as fast and didn't have water squirting through them like today, I could smell the decay, and the burning tooth. After he drilled for what seemed like an eternity, he stopped. His assistant ran some water into a tiny cup in the little sink and told me to rinse and spit. Since he had cut my gum, what I spit was really gross. After that he blew some air into the tooth from a hose, to dry it off, and completed cleaning out the canal down the middle of the root, gave me a chance to rinse and spit again then after drying the tooth he finished cleaning the root canal, and left a hole for the post that would anchor the permanent tooth when it arrived. When he was finished that day he cemented in a temporary tooth. I had to keep the temporary tooth in place until the permanent one arrived. One day while I was eating a peanut butter and jelly sandwich the temporary tooth came out. I just rinsed it off and stuck it back in. Fortunately once my permanent tooth was cemented in place it stayed no matter what I ate.

Time to awake from my daydream and go to my new dentist here in Columbia, Missouri. As I entered the office I noticed immediately the attempt at a peaceful atmosphere, waterfalls on either side of the entrance, a few chairs, some magazines on a table, and a large window looking out to the trees from the waiting area. The receptionist was very sweet and friendly as she gave me the normal papers to fill out. After a short wait, I was escorted back into the office area by a nice girl who introduces herself as Nikki. She wore brightly colored 'scrubs' and smiled pleasantly which helped put me at ease. The chair she led me to is was more comfortable than the one my dentist used back in Pleasant Valley. The room was spacious, and clean. The view through the picture window right in front of my chair was really nice. It overlooked the trees behind the building, and the breeze swayed them in a peaceful motion. I decided that this wouldn't be as bad as I had feared.

The dental assistant entered, and I showed her my baggie. She took an x-ray and a digital picture with a very tiny camera of the top of my tooth, so I could actually see what it looked like close up that added to my feeling that this is a state of the art office. This was an innovation I had never seen before.

When the dentist arrived, we chatted about my dental anxiety and the progress of modern dentistry. He related some of his early experiences with dentists, like the dentist he went to when he was a teenager who didn't have an assistant or receptionist, and would sometimes stop in the middle of working on him to answer the phone. He also told me how the dental picks and drills were soaked in disinfectant solutions similar to combs in a barber shop between patients to kill germs.

He explained that he would have to do a root canal, and put in a post with a new crown, and I said "OK." What else could I say, I need my teeth! He gave me prescriptions for antibiotics (to fight infection), steroids (to keep down any inflammation), and Tylenol with codeine (for pain). I made an appointment right then for the next morning at 9 AM.

Of course, on the way out I had to stop and discuss how I intended to pay for all this with Sherri the office accountant. After my insurance the remaining total bill would be $1000.00. She can set me up with a loan from a company that they deal with which doesn't charge interest as long as you make your payments on time. Since my bill reaches $1000 I would be lucky enough to get a payment plan of little as $55.57 per month for 18 months. This seemed like a good deal, so I took the loan.

When I left I went to Wal-Mart to get my prescriptions for antibiotics and steroids filled, and felt confident that I had made the correct choice for a new dentist.

I was able to keep the worry from my mind during the evening by watching TV.

Tuesday morning I arrived promptly at 9 AM at the dental office and was taken to a room. It was a different room from my first visit, but there was still a large window, this room also included a TV screen that seemed to be suspended from the ceiling! As things were getting set up, I was offered a choice of DVD's to watch. I choose "Raging Bull," expecting that that will keep my mind off my own pain. I was right about that, and the earphones cut any noise from the work being done in my mouth.

As the dentist was giving me the shots of novacaine I realize that the needles hadn't gotten any smaller over the years!

Before he got started drilling he added a "cheek protector" to protect the inside of my mouth, and cheek, that alleviated my usual fear of the drill slipping and drilling a hole through my face. While he was drilling, his assistant kept carefully suctioning the water and whatever else from my mouth, so that I wouldn't choke or drown. It was unlike that horrible suction tube that used to be inserted over my lip into the soft place under my tongue and constantly suck my skin, and make awful noises that I remembered from my teenage years. To keep the tooth area dry, he used a kind of "mouth condom" that protected everything and kept the water and saliva from the tooth, instead of those rolls of cotton that I was used to and that I always thought were going to dislodge unnoticed by anyone and fall into my throat and choke me to death.

When he finished I was fitted for the crown, and given a choice of finishes, I choose gold. I thought it would be nice to have a little "Bling" in my mouth! The movie was pretty much over. I was able to see the whole thing except for one time the assistant was in my way for a few minutes. I made an appointment to go back October 9 to get my new gold crown. The placement of my new gold crown went smoothly. After that I had my teeth cleaned by the hygienist, and spent the winter without any tooth problems. Unfortunately, when spring came more tooth problems followed.

In the spring of 2008 I lost a large filling, in the molar next to the one with the new gold crown, so I called Sterling Dental and returned to the familiar comfortable office. This time I only needed a crown, so not enough time for a whole movie. After the prep work I chose gold again, signed to pay more Care Credit, and wait for the new crown to arrive and be carefully cemented in my mouth. This whole process went without a problem, by spring 2009 my dentist bills were paid as promised and my teeth were working just fine.

The Prize

The mail on that sunny day in March 2008 brought the following promises:

"Bring the key with this flyer to see if you are the winner of the 2007 KIA SPORTAGE. AS A LETTER HOLDER YOU ARE DEFINITELY A WINNER! YOU MAY HAVE WON! $20,000 Cash or a 2007 Kia Sportage GUARANTEED WINNER!"

It was all hard to believe.

Although I didn't win the car or $20,000, I did get a chance on a TV. According to the sales lady the car had already been won. She showed me the board where I could match the "Winning number" on my flyer to the prizes on the board. According to the brochure I had won a choice of World tours, by air, land or sea. It sure sounded nice. As I studied the brochure I discovered my choices were complimentary air fare for two to over 20 spectacular destinations, as long as I paid for between 7 – 14 nights at the hotels they designated. This should have been cause to question the supposed prize, but since I am an optimist I read further, 3 days and 2 nights at a choice of cities sounded good to me. I chose Orlando, Florida, Disney World and Universal Studios, and since I have a friend who lives about 75 miles from there I would combine the prize with my vacation.

I made my reservations for June 18 and 19 and at that time I was charged $50 refundable reservation guarantee. After assurance that I would get it back when I arrived at the Worldwide Travel Center, I agreed. I received the confirmation letter which contained the address of where I was to go. I called the toll free number for better directions and was told it would be easy to find. I headed south imagining that I would find it when I got there.

    The address which I realized wasn't Orlando but Kissimmee wasn't as easy to find as the original operator had told me. After finding the correct street which was the easy part, I stopped at a real estate office to ask directions and was told I was far from my destination but not much more than that. I called the toll free number from my welcome letter and was given another number to call. From that number I was directed to a Ramada Inn about four miles from where I was. The Worldwide Travel Center headquarters was in the back of the Ramada Inn. This should have given me one more clue as to what I was in for. There I was given the paperwork for my hotel room. Since I heard someone mention tickets to Disney World I asked and was told the value of that was $25 so my refund amount was changed from $50 to $75. happily I went to register for my room and at that point I had to pay $12 per night surcharge. After paying I took my luggage to my room and I couldn't get the key card to work, but one of the cleaning staff helped me by unlocking my door for me.

    It was still early, about 3:00, so I headed off to Disney World. The entrance was only about a mile down the street but it seemed about 5 miles into the parking lot. After parking in the lot marked "Dopey" I boarded the tram to the entrance where I would buy what was supposed to be my $25 ticket. It turned out to be $71 for that day for one park, more for the two day pass and still more if I wanted to visit all parks, about $200 total. I never did go back and ask the man in the office what he expected me to get for $25.

I paid my money, got my ticket, and boarded the monorail to the Magic Kingdom. My bags were searched and my fingerprint recorded as I entered.

I had my picture taken with Pluto, saw the show at the magic castle, looked into several shops, saw the hall of president's show for a little air-conditioned relaxation, and then stood in line for about 30 minutes for a boat ride through Africa, India and the Amazon.

Being a little hungry I considered the buffet where I would meet Piglet and Tigger but $32.99 seemed like a large price and it didn't look like Pooh was there that day. At a sandwich shop called Pecos Pete's I purchased an $8 sandwich complete with fries. I found a table and was joined by a friendly couple with a 16 year old daughter and their niece from New Orleans, LA. When I left the restaurant I found that a thunder and lightning storm had just ended. The storm caused the train back to the entrance to be canceled and as it was getting dark I was having a hard time finding my way to the monorail. When I did finally find it there was a delay and I had to wait on the crowded platform. When I found to the tram and the "Dopey" parking lot it was dark. Since things look different in the dark I couldn't find my car. Some very nice people stopped to help me; they drove up and down the rows as I walked. Finally, after I convinced myself it had been stolen, I asked the tram driver to send security over for one last look before I gave up and called the police. Security arrived and I told him I was sure it was the Dopey lot, but I had failed to note which row. We made the circuit up and down the lines of cars while I looked for my car by attempting to set off the car alarm. In a little while I found it where I had left it! I was relieved but also embarrassed as I wound my way back to my motel.

The next morning I was scheduled to listen to the pitch for a time share at 8:30 so that I could get my $75 refund as promised. I was up early and my first hurdle was to get hot water for a shower in my room. I had to call the front desk to find out there was a little brown button to push on the faucet to get the hot water to start. Then after it was the correct temperature you could let go of the button and stand up to shower .

    I arrived at the appointed destination where I had been promised breakfast, that would be welcome since the Ramada Inn didn't provide any complimentary breakfast only a selection of fruits and snacks for sale. I checked in and after a brief wait I met Sergio, who would be my personal salesman. He greeted me warmly and promised we would "have some fun." I rode in his BMW with leather seats and performance tires through an area of very nice apartments, town houses and large homes. As he drove, he was telling me of the only $640 annual grounds fee I would be paying for maintenance when I purchased my time share. We stopped at a nice restaurant near a park. Although the restaurant was nice, I'm not sure I would classify it as 5 star as he did but it had cloth table cloths and cloth napkins. I would call it a 3 star restaurant at best.

    The waitress brought us coffee and orange juice. Breakfast was buffet style with scrambled eggs, plain or with little strips of ham, fried potatoes, bacon and link sausage, and French toast that looked steamed rather than fried. Actually it was so strange looking that Sergio felt he had to point out what it was. There were small pieces of crusty bread, jam and jelly packets, real butter, and some orange or cantaloupe pieces. He admitted to me that it was serving breakfast especially for the time share sales people. I told him I would have enjoyed someplace like Shoney's better because they have more variety. On the ride over and during breakfast Sergio was trying to tell me the benefits of buying a time share. I didn't pay too much attention instead telling him again and again I was only there because I won this trip as a prize and when I decide I want to go on vacation I just get into my car and drive to see my friends and relatives in various states. I really have no interest in a week at some place where I don't know anyone.

After he ate 4 little boxes of cereal and spent several minutes speaking what I think was Spanish during a cell phone call where he was making arrangements to rent a car for his vacation he asked me if I had any money with me. I replied, "I have a couple of dollars in my pocket." He told me I should leave a trip for the waitress. I told him that I thought he should since he brought me to breakfast I ended up leaving $2 by my plate for the waitress.

As he brought me back to the welcome center, he stopped for gas. While I was waiting and since he hadn't opened the windows, I opened the door for air. I noticed reduced rate Disney World tickets. When I mentioned this to him he warned me against them as it was a scam. We returned to the welcome center so I could get my car and follow him to see the time share suites that he wanted to sell me, which he explained would be much nicer than the dump I was staying in now. I replied, "If you wanted me to see how nice they were then that is where I should be staying." He ignored my comment. When we arrived at the time share site he pointed out the wonderful parking structure where you had a covered space for your car. It looked like a regular parking garage to me. After we entered the building and before we looked at one of the suites, he took me to a hallway window and pointed out a new construction site and said, "That is where your time share will be built. I thought, *Does he think I'm a moron?* Then he showed me the spacious model but I explained even though it was very nice it was way to much room for me. I like to visit friends when I vacation. At this point he took me to a large dining room with many tables. As we sat he tried once more to convince me I needed this. The price was somewhere over $20,000, and the terms were $1,500 down and $200 per month for many years. I again told him I was not interested since all my credit cards were maxed out and I was struggling to pay the bills I already had. I thought a little white lie wouldn't hurt and it might shut him up and get my point across so I could get out of there. He left and the next man who arrived I called "The Closer" because I'm sure he was supposed to convince me to sign up. I told him about the tip incident, and his reply was, "Tips for three meals a day would be too much for Sergio to afford." When he went over the price with me I told him "If I had $1,500 I would buy my granddaughter a lap top for school." I also mentioned the state of the economy at which time he asked what church I attended. As the shock from the question wore off, I responded that I didn't think it was his business and he said he would pray for me. He then signed my paper so I could get my $75 back. I asked for directions back to the office and he told me "It is easy just go back the way you came in."

    When I returned to the office I presented my paperwork, got $75 cash and filled out a complaint form about the pray for you statement and the fact that I was told to leave a tip. That distracted me from the small amount ($25) for Disney tickets when they cost 3 times that for one day.

    After I was finished with all that, I headed back to Disney World this time to the Hollywood Films part. I spent about four hours at the park. While I ate a famous Disney Turkey leg I shared a table with a very interesting lady from Virginia who had brought her 12 year old grandson there and was also taking him on a cruise so he would be able to get out and see the world. Her thought was that this would counteract some of his "Red-neckness".

    I enjoyed the time but found I was so exhausted I went back to my hotel room after the big parade and block party with many Disney characters. I dragged myself back to the tram and my parking lot which this time had been the "Goofy" lot. I found my car without a problem. The road out of Disney World seemed to have gotten longer and more complex since I came in.

When I got back to my room, a nice cleaning lady unlocked my door for me and showed me how to turn the key just a little so I would be able to unlock my own door next time. By this time I was so tired that I just lay on my bed and watched TV until I fell asleep.

The next morning I packed up and headed west on Route 4 toward Largo to visit my friend Joanne. Thinking "I will be happy to be away from the insincerity and pushiness of the time share people." At Joanne's I had a nice room, a shower that worked normally, and caring people to have meals with.

Me with Jessica at Stonehenge.

My First Big Trip

It was September 1988 when my good friend Jessica graduated from Vassar College, and enjoyed a long distance romance with David in England. She decided she would like to go see him, and invited me to come along. I had never been out of the country, so I was very excited. We flew to London, England, to visit David, and from there we went to Paris, France, so that Jessica could visit the grave of Oscar Wilde and take a picture for her father who was a great Oscar Wilde fan. We flew from New York City to London, England. I don't remember much about the plane ride, except the seats were narrow, the trip was long, and the movie was Milagro Beanfield War. I remember the movie name, but not much about the movie since I thought it was boring and I guess I dozed through most of it.

At the airport we met David, a nice young man with blond curly hair who was a fun tour guide. After a night's rest at a bed and breakfast just outside of London, we headed west to Stonehenge. I was disappointed to find ropes keeping us away so we couldn't go to the rocks and touch them. Jessica and I did get our picture taken in front of them. That's pretty exciting to look at now, and remember that I was once standing at such a place. According to legends, the beginning of Stonehenge may date back to 8000 BC. Around 2100 BC the Preseli Bluestones were brought from West Wales and aligned to the summer solstice. Preseli Hills is over 250 kilometers (160 miles) away. The larger stones are Sarsen stones from about 40 kilometers (25 miles) away. These stones are the ones you can see in the picture and some are 13 feet high and weigh as much as 25 tons. There is so much folklore about the site it is impossible to tell what is real or not, but the stones are there, and they are big!

From Stonehenge we went on to Holt, England. We stopped there and took pictures because Holt is my married name. Holt was a small town with a grassy square in the center. I don't remember seeing any stores in the town.

Riding around the narrow roads of England in that tiny car, on what seemed to me to be the wrong side of the road was very scary. The roads seemed to be narrow dirt paths between tall hedge rows. Sometimes they were dirt. Even when they were paved, the pavement was brown not black like I was used to. We stopped at Winchester Cathedral, which was breathtaking. Along the way we saw thatched roof cottages. we stopped and walked among giant trees in a forest that reminded me of fairy tales. We stopped and had lunch at a real Pub. Jessica and David began to tease me because I kept saying about everything "It's so old!"

We visited Bath, which had been a spa resort established by the Romans in 43 A.D. [6] According to what I remember the guide said, the area we went into had been Roman baths that had been buried in mud, but excavated by the English. It was amazing to me that they were so old, and were uncovered to show large bath chambers, as large as swimming pools that had been used so long ago.

From there we went to Tenby and South Pembrookshire both in Wales where we visited Pembroke Castle. It was a real old stone castle. Pembrookshire is the area where the Preseli bluestones that are part of the inner circle at Stonehenge came from. While there, we stayed at a bed and breakfast. It had been a family home, but since the owner was a widow she needed to make money so she rented rooms to vacationers. Tenby is

---

[6] date from Wikipedia

along the Atlantic coast so it is a popular vacation area. It was too cold to swim when we were there but the beach looked nice, so we went walking on the sand and took a boat ride out to an island with a ruined castle.

This picture of me was taken in front of the Pembroke Castle in 1988.

We went back to the English coast where we got a ferry across the English channel to Cherbourg on the Normandy Coast of France. On the way Jessica gave David and me some French lessons. The first bed and breakfast we stayed at was the home of a very nice couple who loved Americans because of fighting beside them in various battles during World War II. They didn't speak very much English, but with an English to French dictionary and Jessica's knowledge of French we were able to communicate enough to know what we were talking about. Before we headed inland toward Paris we went to see Mont St. Michel, a church built on a 264 foot high rock formation along the coast of France. According to legend, the archangel Michael appeared to St. Aubert, bishop of Avranches, in 708 and instructed him to build a church on the rocky islet.

Aubert repeatedly ignored the angel's instructions until Michael burned a hole in the bishop's skull with his finger. That did the trick. The dedication to St. Michael occurred on October 16, 708. Mont-Saint-Michael is connected to the mainland via a thin natural land bridge, which before modernization was covered at high tide and revealed at low tide. There is now a causeway connecting it to the mainland.

Getting around France was quite an adventure since David who was driving didn't read French. Jessica had to read the signs and tell him which way to go. We continually passed our turns and had to turn around to try again. This caused them to argue. Sometimes I found it funny and endearing; other times it was annoying. One time we stopped to eat at a restaurant while in France. Since I couldn't actually read the menu I ended up with what seemed to be hot dogs and sauerkraut. Mostly we lived on French bread and cheese during the day. We always stayed at bed and breakfasts so we were fed large hearty breakfasts that kept us going most of the day. At one point while we were in France we didn't have time to do our laundry, so we resorted to turning our underpants inside out!

We decided not to stay in Paris and instead we stayed in a town called Chantilly about an hour by train from Paris. From there we took the train into Paris so we could visit Pére Lachaise Cemetery and get a picture of the grave of Oscar Wilde for Jessica to take back to her father in Brooklyn, New York. Since Wilde's tomb was at the highest point in the cemetery, we had to climb a lot of stairs. While we were at the cemetery we also saw the grave of Jim Morrison and many other famous people, and Jessica got a picture of Oscar Wilde's grave for her father. We also visited the Louvre to see the many beautiful works of art inside and the young artists making chalk drawings on the sidewalk outside. We did stop at a sidewalk café for coffee and pastry before we boarded the train to go back to Chantilly.

Before we left London to return home we did some more sightseeing. We walked across the Thames on the Tower Bridge, and took the tour of the Tower of London. We learned that there is a legend saying "If the ravens ever leave the Tower of London, the White Tower, the monarchy and the entire kingdom would fall." The wings of the ravens are clipped so that they can't fly away. There are either six or ten ravens always around. Many famous people were held and tortured inside the Tower, and many were hanged or be-headed in front of it. We saw the room where Lady Jane Grey was held while waiting to be executed.

While we were in London we also went to Piccadilly Circus which I expected to be a Circus or show with entertainers. Instead it was more like Times Square in New York City, but with statues. After the few days in London, the inside of my nose was black with soot.

I think I must have been so tired that I slept on the entire flight home, since I don't remember it at all.

Over the years I have lost touch with David and Jessica. I still think of them often and the exciting adventures we had together.

Pat Holt

Chicago Trip

I decided to get a ticket to the Pink concert that would be held in Chicago, September 26, 2009. A couple of my friends were going, so I would be able to ride up to Chicago with them. It seemed like a good idea. About a week before the concert they let me know they couldn't go. I still wanted to go so I got a motel reservation for a Best Western very near the concert venue, also very near O'Hare Airport.

I had my plan and started out Saturday morning. In spite of some rain the trip was uneventful. It consisted of traveling on four major highways with each connection clearly marked. As I drove I listened to The 5th Horseman by James Patterson. The transition from Route 55 to Route 294 was marked clearly so it was easy to find, but Route 294 was about 18 miles of busy highway through Chicago, which was marked with signs that were confusing to me. There were three times I had to move over into the far right lane on what looked like an exit ramp to pay a toll. It turned out that just before the third toll was the exit I was supposed to take, but I was so focused on being in the correct lane and not causing an accident I missed my exit. The toll taker was very pleasant, and no doubt I wasn't the first to get confused by all this, she told me how to get to my destination using some city streets after I exited the highway.

The Best Western was very nice and had a choice of restaurants where I could get supper before I walked to the concert. Dinner was ok, the concert was great. Pink sang many of her hit songs, plus a couple of other people's hits. I even met a friendly young lady with her daughter, who are now my Facebook friends. She thought it was wonderful that I came to the concert and wished her mother would do things like that. After the concert I walked back to my motel and began thinking about whether I would stay another night so that I could go into Chicago to sightsee on Sunday or go home. When the desk clerk told me I could get the motel shuttle to the airport and catch a train into the center of Chicago my decision was made.

    Sunday morning I met a friendly man on the shuttle who suggested I visit Millennium Park which was near the train station. The train stop turned out to be about three blocks from Michigan Avenue, the main street of Chicago. The park was truly wonderful. There was a giant shiny object shaped like a bean, I believe it is called "The Bean" because of it's convex surface. As you entered the park, it reflected the sky line that was behind you. I went onto the platform in front of it and took a picture of my reflection, but I came out so distorted I am almost unrecognizable. The park was wonderful but I was getting hungry. I went to the Welcome Center to ask about food and tour choices. I decided to eat at the park and take a tour bus. As I was leaving the Welcome Center, an Asian lady approached me and asked what I had learned at the Welcome Center. I told her about the tour, and she asked if she could join me. I told her yes, so together we found the tour ticket office where we purchased our tickets and got a free tee shirt, which if she hadn't been there to remind me I would have forgotten. From there we went to the outdoor cafe for lunch. During lunch we chatted, she told me her name was Kim, and she was from Korea, had been a seamstress, and did alterations for a famous designer. When she worked, she met many famous people. She lived in New Jersey and commuted into New York City for work. She was home on the day the World Trade Center Towers were hit and watched them fall. Her son had worked in the second tower that was hit. He was among the people who decided to evacuate when the first tower was hit, and although he was covered with ash, he survived. Her daughter and son-in-law were doctors here in Chicago, they wanted her to move to be near them. She bought a condo in Chicago near the park so she could walk around it every day if she wanted. She told me her daughter calls often, and worries if she has enough to eat, but it isn't a problem because there is a grocery store inside the condo building.

During lunch I was thinking about how strange it is for me to have a traveling companion, especially one who I didn't know.

Before we boarded the tour bus she wanted to show me some of the sites in the park that were especially her favorites. The most impressive were the giant faces that were videos of actual people's faces looking and blinking. They make their lips like they were saying "O" and at that time a stream of water shot from their mouths. The faces were shown on something like a flat screen TV with water constantly cascading over them going into a pool between the two faces. Little children were happily playing and splashing in the water between the faces. On the tour bus I learned that the people shown were real people that had each signed a release to have their face shown to the world. We then walked up to see the giant red dinosaur sculpture. From there we found our way to the place where the double-decker tour bus stopped.

We climbed up the tiny circular staircase to find seats on the top deck where we could get a good view of the tall buildings and other interesting sights. The steps of the staircase were so narrow I had to be careful where I put my feet, so that they would fit. As we rode the bus the guide told us about the many historical buildings, such as Al Capone's headquarters, the diamond exchange with an elevator in the center of the building that was large enough for cars, so the diamond dealers would not have to leave their cars until they got to their office door. Of course we saw the Willis Tower (formerly the Sears Tower), Grant Park, where President Obama gave his acceptance speech after being elected President, and Field Museum the home of Sue, the largest/most complete T-Rex. We got off the bus at the Navy Pier where after a trip to the restroom we found the Garrett Popcorn store and got our free sample of their famous "Mix" of Caramelcrisp and Cheesecorn, which the brochure indicates has been a Chicago tradition for 60 years. One box was enough for both Kim and me. I did eat most of mine, but found the Cheesecorn too greasy. My fingernails had an orange hue for days after. While at the pier we went on a boat tour on Lake Michigan. It was a beautiful day for a cruise, and we got a different view of the city sky line, and more city history. When the tour was finished we were offered $20 souvenir pictures of ourselves that had been taken as we boarded. We both passed on the offer. As it was getting near 5:30, which is when the tour busses stop running, we caught the bus back to Millennium Park where we started. That is when I found out that Kim would be celebrating her 80th birthday October 10. We parted ways: she went back to her condo, and I went in search of some authentic Chicago food, either a Chicago Style Hot Dog or Chicago's Original Deep Dish Pizza. After several blocks of searching and asking native Chicagoans' where to get these items, the workers in a Kinko's looked up a Pizza restaurant, gave me directions on a piece of paper and I found Giordano's Pizza. I enjoyed my dinner, even though I had to wait for almost 45 minutes. I could only eat half the pizza, I took the left over with me and gave it to a man who seemed to be homeless and needing food on my way back to catch the train to O'Hare and my motel. I saw a lot in Chicago, there is still a lot more to see. I wish I had gotten Kim's address so I could have maybe kept in touch, and maybe gone to see her again if I went back to Chicago.

The trip out of Chicago was much easier that the trip in, I was more familiar with the exits for toll takers, so I didn't get nervous when I had to get off and on to pay the toll.

Made in the USA
Charleston, SC
19 December 2010